Praise for *Avoiding the Demise of Democracy*

"The practice of true democracy, the participation of an informed electorate in the activities and decision making processes of their government, is and has been in crisis in the United States for decades. Education, practiced by passionate and dedicated teachers and principals, is one of the last great bastions able to protect and pass on the traditions of historically literate citizenship. Unfortunately, public education is very much in crisis, too. It is under attack by the same forces undermining democracy itself, for those forces recognize its power to challenge the status quo and incite change. I have known Sharron Goldman Walker as a friend and colleague for over twenty years. She truly is among our most dedicated and passionate educators. Her cautionary tale deserves to be heard, pondered, and taken seriously. Hers is a voice from the trenches. Her urgency is genuine and just."

—**Michael Harty**, juvenile care worker, Junction City, Oregon

"In her new book, Walker presents the reader important questions about the direction of education today. For example she stipulates that democratic living risks becoming a 'habit of mind,' or end product rather than democracy as a living breathing process that needs to be practiced each day, and more importantly taught in our schools each day. It is this very point many educators working in today's educational environment might argue is not happening. The good teachers and principals Walkers sees as necessary to the survival of democratic education are too often bound by the political wrangling of money and philosophy, typically resorting to the data driven and control models of education. As was her first book *Principals as Maverick Leaders*, *Avoiding the Demise of Democracy* is again a must-read for aspiring teachers and principals and those already in the schools."

—**Gene Biladeau**, middle school teacher, Benson, Arizona

"This book is about the important differences between schooling and democracy. It shows that modeling democracy and allowing it in the classroom, the community, and the administration of schools is paramount if democracy is to survive in America."

—**Sue Cox**, retired high school teacher

"A study of democratic practices in public schools, complete with life experiences and provoking chapter questions. The second of Walker's books exploring the importance of public schools role in society continues Principal Dina Macksy's quest as she challenges, questions, and hammers out some hard truths about schools using historical visitors and current ones. I was on the journey from chapter 1!"

—**Jona Henry**, retired high school teacher

"Democracy in education may not be dead but those who regulate the educational system at both the federal and state levels are focused on holding the pillow of control to its face, suffocating the life out of it, in the pursuit of higher test scores. Dr. Walker understands the fallacy of that approach, recognizing that engagement rather than control is necessary to lead students to take control of their education. Her books should be required reading by all who are involved in the educational system."

—**John Casicato**, retired alternate school teacher

AVOIDING THE DEMISE OF DEMOCRACY

Previous Works by
Sharron Goldman Walker

Principals as Maverick Leaders: Rethinking Democratic Schools
(coauthored with Michael Chirichello, 2011)

AVOIDING THE DEMISE OF DEMOCRACY

A Cautionary Tale for Teachers and Principals

Sharron Goldman Walker

ROWMAN & LITTLEFIELD EDUCATION
A division of
ROWMAN & LITTLEFIELD
Lanham • Boulder • New York • Toronto • Plymouth, UK

Published by Rowman & Littlefield Education
A division of Rowman & Littlefield
4501 Forbes Boulevard, Suite 200, Lanham, Maryland 20706
www.rowman.com

10 Thornbury Road, Plymouth PL6 7PP, United Kingdom

British Library Cataloguing in Publication Information Available

Library of Congress Cataloging-in-Publication Data

Walker, Sharron Goldman, 1945–
Avoiding the demise of democracy : a cautionary tale for teachers and principals / Sharron Goldman Walker.
pages cm
Includes bibliographical references.
ISBN 978-1-4758-0622-9 (cloth : alk. paper)—ISBN 978-1-4758-0623-6 (pbk. : alk. paper)—ISBN 978-1-4758-0624-3 (electronic)
1. Education—Aims and objectives—United States. 2. Democracy—Study and teaching—United States. 3. Democracy and education—United States. I. Title.
LA217.2.W36 2014
370.973—dc23
2013030913

Printed in the United States of America

This book is dedicated to Graham Hunter, the Leeds, Englishman who *always* allowed the facts to interfere with his way of thinking. This book is also dedicated to all educators who realize the importance to America of practicing democracy in education.

CONTENTS

INTRODUCTION

In *Principals as Maverick Leaders: Rethinking Democratic Schools* (Walker & Chirichello, 2011), fictive Principal Dina Macksy travels on a journey of self-exploration hoping to discover why children are sent to school. Through dialogues with people who sit on the shelves of libraries, she discovers that the reason we send our children to school is to preserve democracy.

In this second volume, *Avoiding the Demise of Democracy: A Cautionary Tale for Teachers and Principals*, Principal Macksy returns to the library to explore another question that baffles her. If the product of education is the preservation of American democracy, do principals and teachers guide children in its practice so that when children leave the schoolhouse they will know how to use it?

The book begins with a prologue focusing on the demise of democracy. It tells a tale of citizens of an ancient state who choose to live in freedom. Realizing that they need a governing system that promotes the common good of all citizens, they select democracy as the means to buttress their freedom.

Eventually, their democracy fails because some citizens pursue their personal agendas at the expense of the common good. Principal Macksy calls these citizens Goths, after the nasty and brutish people of the barbarian tribes surrounding their state. Because of the lack of the very excellent teachers and principals needed to guide students in the practice of democracy, the citizens of the ancient state become like the nasty and brutish Goths and the idea of the common good becomes consigned to oblivion.

Each chapter of the book is a dialogue followed by a case study where historians, philosophers, organizational theorists, diplomats, journalists, presidents, pundits, and modern-day educators share views about keeping democracy alive. Specifically, these great thinkers focus on the individual and collective responsibilities of people in a free society.

They ask the reader to consider the nature of American democracy. How do we learn it? What is the quality of the learning? What is the quality of education needed to preserve it? Is the quality of thinking of our educational leaders, the teachers and principals, sufficient to preserve an American way of life? They ask the reader to rethink their own early schooling. Did their teachers and principals practice democracy in the schools they attended?

Concerning themselves with issues of control and reform in the schoolhouse, the participants discuss their impact on the quality of student thinking necessary for a democratic state. In a dialogue that asks who is responsible for the preservation of the American Republic and freedom, the conclusion is that there can be only one answer. Finally, participants demonstrate how very excellent democratic teachers and principals can incorporate democracy in the classroom and schoolhouse respectively.

Each dialogue culminates by posing reflective questions or exercises for the reader in order for him or her to challenge his or her own understandings about education and the practice of democracy in the schoolhouse.

Case studies provide an inspirational narrative that paints a picture for the dialogues. They include a teacher who decides to fight modern-day Goths over a book censorship issue, becoming despondent over the quality of his civility in addressing the issue.

Another teacher relates how he learned the skills of democracy from his position as a city council member and wonders why he did not utilize these skills with his students. A principal engages the reader in an understanding of how teachers enhance their democratic skills as they pass through the day, evolving from Goths who think only of themselves to democratic leaders who consider the education of all their students. A tyro teacher narrates how she unknowingly became a Goth.

A principal relates how control by her teachers led to control of her teachers.

Cognizant that her students weren't learning because she was trying to control them, a teacher thinks about how to exchange her control of the students for active engagement by them. A principal tells the story of how she became a democratic leader by observing how her teachers evolved into democratic leaders in the classroom.

The author—a schoolhouse educator for four decades both in and out of the United States, a Chase Bank Outstanding Principal recipient, a city council member, and author of educational articles and books— believes that education is the key to preserving democracy because it is through education that a common playing field for all people can be found. In addition, she believes that democracy requires an educated, informed populace that schooling does not always produce. Is the practice of democracy in the schools essential for the survival of our social experiment? Principal Dina Macksy asks us to dialogue this exigent question.

The dialogues and case studies in the book are based upon the author's experience as a teacher and principal in the American and British-based West African school systems and upon the authentic experiences of teachers and principals. Many events have been embellished for the purposes of making a point. The school setting and its characters are a fictitious composite of the author's experiences. Any resemblance to real persons is purely coincidental.

Referenced throughout the book are multiple voices that contributed to this work. The words from the voices are cited or improvised from their writings or personal communications.

As noted in *Principals as Maverick Leaders*, although some of the conversations and dialogues between and among the noted experts are embellished and imagined, they are based on the referenced sources. Further references to the same work in the same chapter are not included to avoid redundancy. For that reason, the page numbers in the citations are only included if the statements come directly from a work by the person speaking. The conversations represent the author's perspective of translating theory into dialogues, conversations, and practice without losing the essential understandings of the noted experts whose works are referenced in the text.

Once again, as cited in *Principals as Maverick Leaders*, the author would like to thank all those people who sit on the shelves of libraries, waiting for renewed conversations. And thanks to all the people not on library shelves who took the time to respond to the inquiry—was democracy practiced in the schools you attended? In anticipation, this author thanks the reflective teachers and principals who will think about the practice of democracy in the schoolhouse as a way to avoid the demise of democracy.

SPECIAL FEATURES OF THE BOOK

- Readers are prompted to think about why it is imperative that educators practice democracy in the schoolhouse. If the skills of democracy are not practiced in the schoolhouse, where will students learn them? What will be the quality of the learning? How will that learning impact American freedom?
- Each chapter is written as a dialogue between teachers and the great thinkers of the world. Is it the Goths, the great thinkers ask, who preclude teachers from the practice of democracy in the schoolhouse, fostering their own agenda at the expense of the free exchange of thought? Who are these Goths? What are Goth intentions? How can students, teachers, administrators, and communities keep democracy alive, while preserving public education from incipient Goth inroads?
- Following each dialogue is an authentic case study by a teacher or principal who applies the ideas of the great thinkers to a real schoolhouse situation in which they were involved.
- The book asks teachers and principals to distinguish public schooling from public education and American freedom from American democracy. Will schooling and freedom alone preserve education and democracy?
- Principals and teachers will reflect upon their roles as democratic leaders, guiding students in the practice and process of democracy through modeling and continued practice.
- This book will be useful for aspiring, new, and experienced teachers and principals, as well as professors of education. It will be worthwhile and informative in undergraduate courses in educational phi-

losophy, educational foundations courses, and graduate educational courses in organizational theory, understanding change as a process, educational leadership, pedagogy, and curriculum design.

- Readers are challenged to make decisions from the dialogues and case studies about their responsibilities to the preservation of American democracy as they become cognizant that the links between democracy, freedom, schooling, and education are complex and interwoven in preserving public education and an American way of life. Following each dialogue is a reflection that invites the reader to further his or her understanding of each chapter's conversation.

PROLOGUE

There was once a great state of antiquity called Rome. Its people believed that the ultimate aim in life was happiness. However, they all agreed that to have happiness, one had to be free.

One sunny day in May, the shrill, clear tone of a clarion resounded throughout the great state. The citizens knew that the sound meant that they were to assemble in the large amphitheater, built by the not-so-free people of the state, where they would once again debate a question of the most profound importance. A student, truant from the free public school that all children attended, mounted a platform set up in the midst of the arena, unrolled a scroll, and in a stentorian voice read out to the citizens, "How can we, the citizens of our state, live eternally free?"

There was a disquieting moment as the citizens considered the question. The public school student sat and watched as his elders debated the issues of freedom and the type of government that could underwrite it. He was impressed with the civil manner in which citizens spoke to each other. They didn't have to raise their hands to speak and all citizens listened to each other.

One citizen talked about the natural rights of all people to be free. The people knew that already but because they were a people who practiced civility and mutuality said nothing to disparage the remark. The student made a mental note of this.

Still another person asserted that if men lived freely together, there had to be rules that guided them in the preservation of that freedom.

The student thought about this question, wondering why the people had not written down the rules for their free society. If they had, they would not forget them, he postulated. On the other hand, if each generation did not practice them, they could still forget them. Maybe the citizens had the rules but they had lost them, he concluded.

Another citizen said that freedom for all had its obligations and the people had to protect them. One citizen concluded that in order to be free, each citizen might have to yield some of his freedom in the name of mutuality. The young student, again exercising his mental faculties, took this to mean that no man was completely free when people came to live together. He had to give up something in order to attain something that would profit all. He would gladly give up school to be engaged in such an education as he was now experiencing.

The idea of mutuality kindled minds. We have to have rules to preserve freedom, citizens began to think. "But don't we have them already?" a citizen asked. The student was proud of himself. He was thinking as the citizens, something he rarely experienced in school.

The citizens turned to the student, interrupting his reflections. "Go to the great library of scrolls," they ordered. "Find us those scrolls that would guide us in our freedom." The student, delighted that he was now included in this great group dialogue, dashed off to the library but halfway through his marathon run remembered that the library had burnt down eons ago, along with most of the scrolls in it.

Returning empty-handed, he found the citizens disappointed, but not deterred. They entered a discussion about how they could protect themselves so that freedom for all would be preserved without diminishing what they already had.

"Why not look at the states surrounding us," the student offered, feeling comfortable to speak now that he had witnessed the civic virtue that permeated the citizens in the amphitheater. There were no hectoring teachers in this crowd, he reflected.

An elder citizen, proud that the student had asked his question, said that those who lived around them, the Goths and other affiliate tribes, were nasty and brutish people whose leaders were equally nasty and brutish. Goth leaders looked for ways to enrich themselves, were licentious, and cared little for the people. So the citizens rejected outright these guides. They could teach them nothing about how to preserve freedom since the Goths and other affiliate tribes had none.

However, they did concur that one disinterested citizen might have the ability of making the decisions for all the people. But where could such a person, who would put the public interests above his own, be found?

They thought about this question, which of course prompted other concerns. A citizen stated that if they chose one person of great sagacity to lead them, this wise person would have to isolate himself from others who would try to unduly influence him at the expense of the people. Of course, he could find residence in the ivory tower that had once housed those who contemplated exigent cosmological, morphological, and epistemological issues, but his very isolation would make him forget what it was like to be of the people. As the citizens weighed the issues, the student noted that they were cognizant of the nature of people and projected this philosophy in their discussions.

As the citizens ruminated and pursued further debate, they all agreed that the system of governance that would best protect their freedom was a system of governance called democracy, which to them meant rule by the people. They concurred that in a democracy there would be times when they would have to surrender their private interests for the public interests of all.

They deemed it necessary to inscribe these words, *rule by the people*, on a giant boulder so that all could always see these words and refer to it for guidance in times of obliviousness. The not-so-free people chiseled these words on the rock and then rolled it to the top of a hill. As the people gazed up and admired the etched words, *rule by the people*, they took scant notice of the not-so-free people who were doing all the physical heavy lifting.

For a time, the people were happy. But since the citizens were reflective and critical thinkers, another question was posed. Hearing the sound of the clarion, they again gathered in the amphitheater. The student, again truant from school, took to the platform and called out the new question. "How do we keep our democracy alive? How do we protect our freedom from those very few citizens who do not want to consider the public interests of all?" The citizens thought this question salient because it became noticeable that a few people had begun to engage in profligate and venal activities at the expense of the public good.

After much debate, discussion, negotiation, and persuasion, the citizens created rules concerning the rights of all people. The rules were about the freedoms that the citizens could exercise without fear of punishment. Women and the not-so-free people were not included in the rules and so did not enter the dialogues. The student made a mental note of this, thinking that although this was true, the new system of government and the new rules provided a means for the government's self-improvement.

The citizens now concurred that their rules were fair because they guaranteed freedom for *all* men and democracy for *each*. Again, the not-so-free people chiseled the rules about the protected freedom of citizens on the boulder atop the hill just under the definition of democracy. Each year, teachers would lead their classes up the hill to remind the children of the rules that underscored their freedom and kept democracy alive.

"But would class trips be enough?" a citizen inquired. "Simply telling the children the rules without practicing them from generation to generation has its pitfalls," said another. The student reflected upon this question. After all, he was in the best position to know the answer to their queries.

"I have now learnt how one goes about creating a democracy," he told the citizens from his position on the platform. "You have allowed me to be part of the process. But students in the classroom will just hear the story told by their teachers or read about it in the library scrolls. They will have no practice in its meaning as I have had. They will not know how to keep democracy alive."

"The student is right," observed a citizen. "If our children do not know how to do democracy, how will our citizens protect themselves from becoming like those nasty and brutish people around us? How will we avoid the demise of democracy?"

So they brainstormed the questions they would need to answer in order to avoid the demise of democracy and protect their citizens from becoming like the nasty and brutish people around them.

"How do we preserve democratic living from one generation to another?" a citizen asked. "How might we assure ourselves that democracy will not become a habit of mind? Are more than field trips necessary for children to become democratic citizens? Who is responsible for the preservation of democracy in our state?"

They again agreed that education was the answer to all these questions. "Democratic preservation and enlightenment will depend upon the quality of the mental processes of our children," said a citizen. "That is why very excellent leaders as teachers and principals will be necessary to guide their thinking and avoid the demise of democracy." They all agreed that, through education, the greatest experiment in free government the ancient world had ever seen would survive.

"But we are not educated in the schools," the student remarked without trepidation. "We are only *schooled*. Because you have included me in the practice of democracy, I have been educated. But tomorrow when I return to class, I will continue to be schooled. Why isn't schooling educative? Why can't my school practice what I have witnessed today?"

The citizens listened to the student and in unison said that they would have to staff the schools with very excellent democratic leaders as teachers and principals who knew how to model and practice with students the democratic way, avoiding the demise of democracy. But they also said that they did not desire to eliminate what worked for the students now. "We just have to make it better," they agreed.

"But do we have very excellent democratic leaders as teachers and principals who know how to do this and can teach it to our children, avoiding the demise of democracy?" asked a citizen. A disquieting silence descended upon the amphitheater.

And as the question was held in limbo, generations of children grew, graduating from their schools and assuming their adult roles in society. A time came when the more discerning citizens of the state perceived that not everyone championed this novel idea of citizens ruling themselves. They saw some citizens slowly becoming Goth-like, proposing changes to the state that seemingly benefited all men but really benefited only them. But still, those who proposed the Goth-like changes agreed to uphold the rules chiseled on the boulder atop the hill while furtively doing the opposite of what they said.

More timed passed and more citizens became dubious about the effectiveness of their rules on the boulder atop the hill. "Why, good citizens, are some of us abandoning the rules?" it was asked. "Because," answered a citizen, "this democracy of ours requires much more than ordinary states require. It requires that each of us be vigilant and guard the state against those who would take it from us. Some citizens have not yet learned that our freedom demands that we balance our own interests with the interests of the state in order to avoid the demise of democracy. They work furtively to enhance their own interests."

"Yes, democracy does require an enlightened mindset," a citizen reflected, "Students must be taught how to expand the limits of their own thinking to incorporate the welfare of all the people as well as themselves."

And again the question was asked, "But do we have the very excellent democratic leaders as teachers and principals who know this and can practice it with our children, avoiding the demise of democracy?"

There was again silence in the amphitheater because no one knew the answer to that question.

"Democracy requires civic virtue and mutuality," remarked a citizen, bypassing the question. "It requires each of us, at times, to put away our private interests in order to pursue public ones. Democracy is about the common good. Democracy requires the practice of it in the schoolhouse so that the quality of our children's mental processes will determine the state's democratic growth. . . ."

"Not the right answers on a tablet," the student added. "But do we have the very excellent democratic leaders as teachers and principals who know this and can practice it with our children?"

"If we don't," echoed a citizen, "when some create rules only for self-profit, we will not always know it because democracy will morph into a process learned through osmosis. Eventually more and more citizens will become like the Goths, permeating our society and proposing laws that will profit only them at the expense of the common good. Without the practice of democracy in the schools, the good citizens will not know what is happening to them."

"This will not happen," a citizen answered, "as long as the words on the boulder atop the hill do not become a habit of the mind and are practiced every day, at every level, in our schoolhouses by the very excellent teachers and principals."

And so generation after generation passed and students were led up the hill to read the words on the boulder. Leading them were their teachers and principals.

But because the children did not discuss the ideas and practice the rules in their schools, slowly and stealthily the interests of the few became valued over the interests of the many. With this erosion of democracy came the erosion of civic virtue and mutuality. Civil dialogue transmuted into specious arguments. The citizenry became corrupt as many began to think of the state as a mere appendage of themselves, furthering their own self-aggrandizement.

Finally, the great ideals upon which the citizenry had built their state eroded as they became increasingly like their neighbors, the Goths. Then one day in May, they became the Goths and the boulder rolled down the hill, crushing them. It sat alone and unclaimed in the middle of the amphitheater. The citizens could no longer avoid the demise of democracy because the very excellent democratic leaders as principals and teachers were never found.

Dialogue 1

JUST WHO ARE THE MODERN-DAY GOTHS?

Principal Dina Macksy began the day doubting whether principals and teachers could ever practice democracy in the schoolhouse. Democracy was doomed if it wasn't practiced, she rued, and America would be crushed just like the ancient state of Rome.

Walking from classroom to classroom, she witnessed similar events: teachers schooling rather than teaching, students sitting quiescently, rather than learning. Returning to her office, she received the telephone call from the teacher at Hatchery High School, referencing the Goths.

Feeling despondent about what she was seeing and hearing, the principal retreated to the public library where she sought refuge in the *Voices Across Time* seminars. As organizer of the seminar series, she could invite any number of guests lying restive in their tomes to join her in a discussion about why the practice of democracy was not evident in the classroom.

Elated at the opportunity to extricate themselves from their cramped space on the shelves, her guests were always on call to offer up whatever knowledge they had concerning the questions Dina posed. Today, as she entered the library, those whose services she required anxiously gazed down upon her, following her quick stride to the round table with its large, open center that she always had ready for them. They soared through the air, diaphanous figures of all body types, lines of experience etched into their countenances, from this stack and that stack over and through the multi-subject labyrinth of the library and floated gently down to the capacious seating around the table.

The walk-in patrons of the library, sitting quietly at the wooden rectangular tables, felt a faint flutter of air pass over them as Principal Macksy's guests drifted away from their space on the shelves. Looking up from their reading, their eyes skimmed the area in a vain attempt at locating the sudden movement of air. Not seeing anything, they returned their eyes to the pages before them. People are no longer curious, Dina thought.

The wizened librarian, her pince-nez clipped tightly to the bridge of her nose, hurriedly dashed over to the figures, her spindly hands holding their nametags. "Please write your names and professions on these cards before taking your seats," she directed each of them in a muted voice, not wanting to disturb the walk-in patrons of the library.

As the guests seated themselves, Dina began her salutation, abruptly putting an end to their felicitous chatter. "As you can see, ladies and gentlemen, seated at our table are distinguished voices from across time. Some of you, like philosophers Plato and Cato, have been housed here for decades. Some of you—like historian and Pulitzer Prize recipient Gordon S. Wood; teacher, principal, superintendent, and college professor Michael Chirichello; and Nobel laureate Huerta Mueller—continue filling the stacks with knowledge and wisdom. And some of you just come and go, borrowing from the past while building bridges to the future. But all of you have been summoned once again to renew an understanding of freedom and democracy and its relationship to education and schooling.

"Does anyone listen anymore to what you have to say?" she asked the circumspect gatherers assembled at her table. "Or is it an ineluctable fact of fate that you are forgotten by most, the dust on your tomes elevating with time? Will America's social experiment in democracy fail if your ideas remain entombed in your tomes, no longer exhumed for reflection, discussion, or debate?"

"The participants who come and go from the bits and bytes floating throughout the air are now here, Principal Macksy," the librarian announced, interrupting the principal. "As soon as they solidify, I'll distribute their name tags. They take a little longer to settle. And I will watch for the casual walk-ins who are not here as library patrons, but wish to contribute to the conversation at the seminar table."

Completing her task, the spindly librarian slowly and stiffly lumbered from the room to attend to her other patrons having told Dina that there was a space at one section of the table that troubled her. "I am not able to know if those seats contain guests or not," she said pointing with her long, thin index finger to a location at the round table far removed from the others.

"Something occupies that space at one time and then at other times does not," she whispered, fingering the metal portion of the pince-nez and carefully lifting it from the bridge of her nose. Her eyes squinted and her head leaned forward in the direction of the area she was describing. "What I mean is I think I am able to discern amorphous forms which at times distend and at other times contract. Every now and then, the nebulous forms appear to metastasize into something more than they are. At present, I even think I hear their voices, but cannot detect what is actually being said. I think they are singing about war and science and something that sounds like rules, but I cannot be certain. Their words are as convoluted as their forms."

Fingering the part of her eyeglasses where the frame meets the lens, Dina looked closely at the space, seeing only emptiness. She did notice that some of her guests avoided the area. However, not seeing or hearing anything, she turned her attention to her guests, speculating that the wizened librarian was perhaps in need of a restive retreat, more contemporary spectacles, or an audiologist.

Seated next to Dina was a small, slope-shouldered man who was not from the shelves, not a byte from the air or a casual walk-in, although his cadaverous flesh and thinning white-yellow hair gave him an appearance of being older than he actually was.

"Today's special guest is Mr. Trey Pidation, a history and English teacher from Hatchery High School," she announced to the group. "Today, Mr. Pidation telephoned me. He said that he was apprehensive about speaking to me openly when I attended his school as a member of a school accreditation team. He feared that I might be a Goth."

"I have seen teachers like him before," Principal Macksy sighed, scanning the multigenerational assemblage of people sitting at her round seminar table, "teachers too apprehensive to speak to me openly, and meeting in the shadows of dark corridors to say what they couldn't say in the light. So I listened with rapt attention to Mr. Pidation as he spoke to me. He described education as a Procrustean bed prepared by those he called Goths.

"'They see the schoolhouse as instruments for their own purposes. These agents of delusion are everywhere,' he warned me, 'chipping away at our social and political foundations while Americans, and in particular, educators, sleep.'"

"They do sleep, Principal Macksy," cautioned a man wearing a three-piece suit, the jacket having exaggerated shoulder pads. He also wore, as did the librarian, rimless spectacles attached to the bridge of his nose. A trim mustache in the shape of a chevron spread across his upper lip. His nametag identified him as John Dewey, philosopher. "Mr. Pidation is no crackpot, Principal Macksy, as you first thought," he counseled in a whisper to the principal.

"These Goths he talks about, ladies and gentlemen," Mr. Dewey said, his voice more audible now as he addressed his audience, "are the nebulous forces weaving their way in society, oppressing liberty, and disseminating distrust in order to accomplish their own agendas."

As he spoke, his eyes focused at the section of table that had so flummoxed the wizened librarian. "They chip away at our democracy in subtle ways. As society 'becomes more interwoven and complex, they can hide in deeper layers and weave their way insidiously throughout it'" (Ratner, 1939, p. 721).

"The Roman Empire, Mr. Dewey, made it easier for the intrusion of the Germanic tribes to slowly chip away at the great Republic," effused Mr. Trey Pidation, eager to share his knowledge of history with rapt listeners, "and to finally decimate it. But it wasn't the tribes that led to the Roman state's demise. The Roman state imploded from within as the citizens became lazy and corrupt (Wood, 2011). They were far more interested in what they could do for themselves than what they could do for themselves and the people. They forgot that being a democracy meant knowing that as you nourish yourself, you nourish your community as well. The Romans became the people they didn't start out wanting to be.

"But now, as Mr. Dewey indicated, the modern-day Goths are more sophisticated at deluding us into believing what they want us to believe," he continued. "Look at them!" he suddenly erupted, his face flushing with passion, the tremulous fingers of one hand stretched outward. "They sit at this very table chanting about war and the decimation of those who oppose them!"

The guests followed the direction in which his fingers pointed, but only a few could discern anything credible. Feeling defeated, Mr. Pidation sighed heavily, sinking back in his chair.

"They are there, I tell you," Mr. Pidation said numbly. "You just can't see them because they do not yet want you to see them. But like modern-day snake oil salesmen, they delude us into believing that their way is the only way to save our Republic from imploding!"

A disquieting feeling suffused the table as the participants waited for Mr. Pidation to regain his composure. Then turning away from the amorphous figures he saw, the teacher retreated back to the figures at the table, explaining that he had met Principal Macksy two weeks ago when she had visited his school as a member of an accreditation team evaluating his school's performance but had feared talking to her face-to-face.

"I called Principal Macksy because I did not think she was a Goth," he explained. "She did not appear to be like so many out there pushing their desultory educational plans upon us. It appeared to me that she was trying to understand why schools ignore the practice of democracy, so crucial to preserving our freedom and the democratic experiment. She was trying to understand why educators were not demanding that they, themselves, practice democracy in the schoolhouse."

"Thank you, Mr. Pidation," Principal Macksy said gratefully, "but I must candidly admit that at first I thought that you were just another teacher who cowers in corners, acting the part of the sycophant each time you met with school leaders, too timorous to tell me what was really on your mind. Of course, after talking with you I find that we both believe that each schoolhouse has to be conceived as a social arrangement where people live together for part of a day. When people live together, who should make the decisions for them? Should it be all the people, some people, or one person? Most people enter the school-house and think *so what do I do now?* There is no *we* in the *I* (Etzioni, 1983).

"So I share your anxiety, Mr. Pidation, about the future of our na-tion's experiment in democracy, because democracy is a *we*," the princi-pal continued. "I do not see educators building together the capacity of students to learn how to live together democratically. Have educators allowed democratic living to become a habit of mind (Lees, 1995), oblivious to the fact that democracy is a process, not a product? It is my belief that only in a school setting do we have the most opportunity to engage and reengage in building the capacity of *associative living* (Hansen, 2006) that is required of us if our democratic experiment is to continue and is not taken for granted."

"It is indeed in the schools that children have the most opportunity to be guided in the best forms of the kind of reflective communication necessary for associative living," noted educator Lucile Lindberg (1954). "Because children live with others in the world, others must be considered in the process of locating, identifying, and developing their individual needs. It is through the practice of cooperative living that children become aware of those individual needs. Equipped with this knowledge they can continuously improve their methods of thought and reflection. This process of working together in order to build their individual critical thought must start from the moment the child enters the schoolhouse."

"I don't see that people work together in the schoolhouse and if they do, it certainly must happen on an unconscious level, Ms. Lindberg," said Mr. Pidation mordantly. "From the start of the child's education, I don't think the practice of working together is built into the schoolhouse. We forget that, as you suggested, democracy is a group process, a social one. It is in the group that we define who we are while simultaneously learning who others are. But because we don't practice democracy or even think about practicing it, we don't recognize that our patterns of behavior are being worked out by others, not by ourselves."

"Others do sway great influence over us," Principal Macksy agreed. "But if educators were more practiced in the skills of critical thought, cooperation, bargaining, and accommodation, perhaps they would not be so easily swayed. I rarely see students exercising these skills in the classroom or teachers at faculty meetings. People just don't trust each other enough to take risks and attempt cooperation. They haven't been practiced in this. But these skills can only be developed in an educative environment where people can take risks and learn the value of human dignity. Unfortunately, they cannot take risks when there is only a modicum of trust and human dignity is not fostered."

"I thought Mr. Pidation spot-on," Principal Macksy told the assembled group at the round table. "Goth reformers would have us all lie in one Procrustean bed . . . cutting us all down to one size as Mr. Huxley (Huxley, 1932) described in his dystopia, *Brave New World*."

"Quite correct you are, Principal Macksy," the author of the book shouted from his seat at the table. "At my Central London Hatchery and Conditioning Centre, those in power can create any kind of a cog necessary to propagate a happy society. And because cogs have no awareness that their happiness has been chosen for them by powerful people who keep them in their fated place, there are few societal disruptions. I have created the brave new world where the minds of men are not addled with complex thought. They are civil to each other and quite content."

"We are easier to control, Mr. Huxley," Principal Macksy affirmed, "when people are more alike than different . . . when there is little variation among and between them. But to fit us into the Procrustean bed, those whom Mr. Pidation calls Goths have to insist on programs in the school that drain children of their creativity, spontaneity, and intellect."

"'Indeed in their first appearance,' interrupted Mr. Dewey, 'and in the early stages of operation,' these modern Goths are likely to be 'welcomed for some obvious advantages they bring with them—possibly as a promise of greater freedom' (Ratner, 1939, p. 721). It is deplorable how easily the public accepts their chicanery!"

"Indeed, Mr. Dewey, it is deplorable," Mr. Pidation conceded. "As a teacher, I do what I am told by the Goths, although that was not always the case." Turning his face toward Principal Macksy, he asked if she, too, always follows blindly as he does now. But before giving Dina an opportunity to reflect, he continued his line of thought.

"Schools are not analogous to the business industry, ladies and gentlemen. The product a business produces is a cog, to be sold for a price. The product a school produces should be a democratic citizen, capable of making informed decisions about the path our great nation takes in order to maintain our freedom. Can that be sold for a price? The modern Goths think that it can.

"Children spend their most informative years being schooled in the same way as cogs are produced in the factory," Mr. Pidation decried. "They are passed along in assembly line fashion from one grade to the next by soporific teachers who pour information from prosaic textbooks into their heads. At the terminus of the assembly line, they receive fill-in-the-blank bubble tests that they must pass so that society can acclaim, with aplomb, that it has done its job of educating them. The Goths systematically plan it this way.

"The only way we protect ourselves against the Goths is through an educated citizenry," the teacher concluded, "but education does not happen when children are merely schooled in how to take tests and not nourished in how to build the intellectual muscle that democratic governance demands. The founding fathers knew this and that is why they advocated an educated citizenry."

"Indeed, we did just that," declared the third president of the United States, Thomas Jefferson. "I recall a letter I wrote to my colleague George Wythe in 1786. The letter exhorted that the university movement be firmly established. I wrote to him that 'I think by far the most important bill in our whole code is that for the diffusion of knowledge among the people. No other sure foundation can be devised for the preservation of democracy and happiness. Preach, my dear sir, a crusade against ignorance. Establish and improve the law for educating the common people. . . . The tax [that] will be paid for this purpose is not more than the thousandth part of what will be paid to kings, priests, and nobles who will rise up among us if we leave the people to ignorance'" (Honeywell, 1931, pp. 12–13).

"Your belief, Mr. Jefferson, that the people could easily nourish a democratic system of government can only become a reality if the schools practice the prerequisite skills of democratic association," Mr. Pidation insisted. "I sometimes don't think I even know what living in a democracy means anymore, not having been practiced in it in my own early schooling. Maybe the preeminent American Revolution scholar, Gordon S. Wood, can tell us why the founding fathers went to so much bother to give us something that we take for granted."

"I shall be glad to," said Mr. Wood (1998). As he adjusted his body to the contours of the chair, Dina could not help but notice that the historian did not suffer the ashen look on his countenance that some of the other participants wore, perhaps, because he was still of an age where he could contribute further tomes to the stacks. "For the founding fathers, democratic republic meant rule by the people," he began. "In fact, as Thomas Paine said, the word *republic* meant the public good or the good of the whole. Therefore, the system rests upon majority rule, with the rights of minorities safeguarded through systems negotiated and inscribed in the Constitution.

"The sacrifice of individual interests to the greater good of the whole forms the essence of the new republic," he continued. "Up until this time, the error of existing governments had been the sacrificing of the public good to the private greed of a small ruling group or to one particular person. But the founding fathers knew that the American people were linked together in communities and formed a kind of organic relationship. What was good for the whole community was ultimately good for all its parts.

"In a republic," Mr. Wood mused, "each man must be persuaded to submerge his personal wants into the greater good of the whole. For example, he must be willing to volunteer for military service or serve on public committees without pay as the founding fathers did."

As he spoke, the historian glanced at the section of the table where the nebulous forms seemed to be and could not help but notice that their glinting eyes and jittery forms were in a superagitated state, shuffling about in the discrete space they occupied.

"It is the responsibility of the schools to develop the individual who can place his public interests above his private ones, Mr. Wood, because schools are social organizations," Principal Macksy advanced. "I learned from Ms. Lindberg that when we work with others, we are more apt to identify our own needs as well as the needs of others. But as a principal, I find it difficult sometimes to think and enact democracy because of all the fads, trends, and reforms deluging the schoolhouse."

"We, as a society, cannot extricate ourselves from fads and nostrums, Principal Macksy," educator Diane Ravitch reminded her, "'unless we carefully look at how we got entangled in them in the first place. We will continue to chase rainbows unless we recognize that they are rainbows and there is no pot of gold at the end of them'" (Ravitch, 2010, p. 12).

"That may be true, Ms. Ravitch, but as Principal Macksy alluded to, the schools are unfailingly inundated by a deluge of new prescriptions from outside their walls," Mr. Pidation said, exasperated. "They are sometimes forced upon us by those above us who think that, with this one new prescription, our schools will be cured of what ails them and there will be the pot of gold. So once again we immerse ourselves in an idea that teachers and principals know won't work.

"To develop disinterested citizens—people who put their concerns for the common good above their private motivations—Ms. Ravitch," he argued, "children must learn and practice their habits every day that they are in school so that they can more adroitly question as well as answer.

"Unfortunately, all the school system wants are high scores on state tests," he rued, "and teachers are compelled to program students for those tests. For example, English teachers at my school created a fail-proof writing template so that the average student could confidently write an expository essay for the state test. The students followed the pattern faithfully but still the scores were average. In the teachers' lounge, we pondered what the state wanted, just as students pondered what their teachers wanted, in order to excel.

"One of my colleagues, an English teacher, told me," Mr. Trey Pidation continued, "that after years of pushing and modeling, she became discouraged because the kids did exactly what the state required. There was no fun, spontaneous, creative writing. But the teachers delivered what the state required of them, while the students were flummoxed at the sense of it all, as were the teachers. They didn't question the work being done, Principal Macksy. They just did it.

"Writing for our students became a fill-in-the-blank chore and was mediocre at best. Some teachers did feel that the guidelines for writing were valuable because they gave teachers defined guidelines. But when the system perfected its requirements, originality and uniqueness were ground out. I still remember the kids looking at the teachers as if we had betrayed them. Only the superintendent was happy. He didn't see their faces. He just saw the passing scores in the newspaper."

"Even if he did see their faces, would it have mattered?" Dina asked herself. Turning to Mr. Dewey, she asked, "Is the purpose of schools just to prepare students to pass a test and allow administrators to climb ladders based upon the results of these tests? Or is it, as you suggested, to prepare a person to enter society with the ability to think critically and appreciate the divergent views of others, and to demonstrate compassion, independent work habits, and sound judgment? Are not those the qualities with which a person should be imbued if our republic is to survive?"

"They certainly are," he agreed. "Democracy is in education where these attributes are developed and practiced, in the company of others, as Ms. Lindberg proposed. Democracy is a way of life: one learns it through living with others. It is a process that never ends in its development as a society freely interacts and debates issues regarding the welfare of each individual and thus all individuals. It is within this debate that we grow both morally and intellectually (Dewey, 1916, 1938).

"Yet I find it difficult to believe after so much time has passed," he continued, "that people both in the schoolhouse and out of the schoolhouse do not understand that in order to preserve democracy and further these attributes, they must practice democracy and forgo having children sit with their hands folded and waiting to be told what to do."

"And the permanent struggle for the creation of a democratic community perpetuates itself only if these beliefs and values are tenaciously held by the people," added Mr. Trey Pidation. "Our democratic ideals are the glue that holds the American people together. The Goths clandestinely work to loosen this adhesive and replace it with their own in order to serve their own interests and purposes.

"History has demonstrated that autocracies are held together," he explained, "by the control of a minority and enforced by the armies that the minority commands. Armies don't always have to wear uniforms. I see those powers of the modern-day Goths sitting quietly at the table. I see their snake oil salesmen, their agents of delusion, in the schoolhouse and out of the schoolhouse obeying their orders! I know this, but do nothing about it.

"In fact, I am ashamed of myself as an educator," he admitted disconsolately, "because I know that the latest round of political mandates imposed on the schools will do little if anything to shape character, teach children how to work together, and foster their intellectual growth. I know that each of these mandates chips away at our democratic foundations.

"Yet, like a martinet, I race in rhythm with the other minions, following orders, doing what I am told to do, although resenting it, yet doing what I resent. The students resent it; I resent it; yet, I do nothing to challenge my orders. I am not a cog. Why don't I know how to work with others and rise above my cog status? Why do I behave as if I were bred in the Hatchery?

"Don't you ever feel, Principal Macksy," he asked, his eyes again fixed on the amorphous forms he watched sitting at the table, "that you have become just another martinet of the agents of delusion, these

Goths, following futile mandates where students sit for those state tests that the voters believe will make the nation's children smarter? But smarter for what? Have we lost sight of who we are as a nation?"

"Somehow our nation got off track in its efforts to improve education," Ms. Ravitch chimed in. "'The accountability movement replaced what once was the standards movement. What was once an effort to improve education turned into an accounting strategy: measure, then punish, or reward'" (Ravitch, 2010, p. 16).

"'Good education cannot be achieved by a strategy of testing children, castigating educators, and closing schools. That is what happens when schools fail to live up to the expectations of the test instead of the expectations of democracy'" (Ravitch, 2010, p. 112).

"What happens is that educators become me, Ms. Ravitch," Mr. Trey Pidation lamented. "I feel sometimes like I have moved into Mr. Hobbes's state of Leviathan. I have made a pact with the devil, accepting the tyranny of control just to keep my sanity and do my job. I am so confounded as to what my duty is. Is it to my school or is it to the principles upon which this country was built?"

"I did say, in the sixteenth century," interjected political philosopher Thomas Hobbes (1996), his black garments and pale countenance contributing to his cold, hostile appearance, "that when the social agreement between the state and the populace is no longer valid, the people have the right to take action. The school is a microcosm of the society in which you live. Men are nasty and brutish. They must be controlled. I say tear the school down!"

"But I do not want to tear it down!" railed Mr. Trey Pidation. "American public education allows every child the free right to be educated. Such a system should be cherished since not all countries believe in a free education for all children. But our educational system and our social institutions have become so intellectually malnourished. What has been consigned to oblivion is that within the bureaucratic structure of schools are people who interact with each other and things and from these interactions form new experiences which integrate and form new thought (Dewey, 1938). Should not this integration be guided by educators who *can* guide?"

"We have also failed to recognize that 'there are no quick fixes or perfect educational theories,'" school superintendent Carl Cohn advised. "'School reform is a slow, steady, labor-intensive process' that depends on 'harnessing the talent of individuals instead of punishing them for noncompliance with bureaucratic mandates and destroying their initiative. We cannot quantify solutions as so many would have us do'" (Ravitch, 2010, p. 66).

"Democracy is pragmatic, Mr. Pidation," Ms. Ravitch added. "Ideas and solutions cannot be tested against a rigid ideology but tried in the real world where they can be argued over, changed, accepted, or debated just as we are doing now."

"But the schools are controlled by the ideologues, not the pragmatists, Ms. Ravitch," Mr. Trey Pidation warned. "The Goths sit there, watch us, and want us to forget that democracy is pragmatic. Their sole objective is to reshape America as they want it to be. They don't want to tear the schools down either; just remake them in a way that will prepare students for their hatchery where everything is quantifiable!"

"I know those men well," said political pundit Abraham Bishop, popping up in his chair, elated that he now had his opportunity to articulate the conjurers of political delusion that he had decried in his 1801 oration on the extent and power of political delusion in New Haven, Connecticut, at the inception of America's experiment in democracy.

"These people who sit over there have 'engaging manners, act holy, meek, honest, and patriotic,'" he bellowed, the full force of his words aimed at the suspicious space at the table, "'but are only interested in their own welfare, not in the common good of Americans. They are all around us, acting with their powers of fabrication, their sagacity in schooling, and success in securing fit instruments for their purposes'" (Bishop, 1801, p. 8).

"You, Principal Macksy, have seen them yourself," he continued, standing up, his arms and hands gesticulating in the direction of the amorphous forms. "These are the contemporary politicians who convince Americans that testing is the way out of the school crisis and have made, as Ms. Ravitch indicated, the testing program more important than the learning itself.

"These are the school leaders who have placed schooling as a higher priority than education. These are the religious proselytizers who want God in the schoolhouse—and only their God. These are the overzealous parents who charge into school and demand that children not be exposed to certain books because it offends their illiberal beliefs. These are the puppet administrators who carry out the initiatives because they want to keep their jobs. These are the teachers who are comfortable doing what they are told.

"'The object of delusion,'" he shouted, floating up and onto the table, "'is to gain the wealth, honors, and favors of men, by cheap, false, and insidious means. I fear that the ill-informed public does not have the reason to apprehend the political chicanery of those pursuing their individual agenda at the expense of the common good of the people'"(Bishop, 1801, p. 8).

"They lack reason, Mr. Bishop, because critical thought is not encouraged. Teaching students to reason takes time away from focusing on the state test," Mr. Trey Pidation rued, content now that he had an ally at the table that saw what he saw at the suspicious section of the table. "When our country was young, I tell my students, Mr. Bishop, that the common people were rough and lacking formal schooling, having little awareness of the world. Sometimes I think we want to keep them in that stage of evolvement. Ignorant people are easier to control."

"And that is why we must educate our children," explained Thomas Jefferson.

"Yet, Mr. Jefferson," Principal Macksy said, bitterness permeating her tone, "more and more I see the schoolhouse taken over by the benighted masses who impose their ineffective demands, mandates, and simplistic explanations as the cure for schools without understanding the problems and without knowing that each schoolhouse is different and as such has different needs.

"Schools may look the same on the outside," she continued, "but just like people, something unique defines each one. Harvard president James Conant (1959) suggested that schools should be improved school by school."

"'If I have made myself clear,'" Mr. Conant affirmed, "'it will be evident that there is no such thing as a typical American high school. Furthermore, it is impossible to draw a blueprint of an ideal high school. . . . Schools do have to change one by one'" (p. 97).

"It's all about control, Principal Macksy," Mr. Pidation cautioned. "The Goths and their snake oil salesmen want us to have as little variation in thought as is possible. They want control and they train us through a system of rewards and punishment, just as Pavlov did with his dogs. As Ms. Ravitch indicated, we receive rewards for good performance and are castigated for a poor one.

"Good teachers, whose students have high scores on state tests," Mr. Pidation further elaborated, "receive merit pay. Good schools, with high test scores, receive accolades in the newspapers. Good textbooks are those that take diversity out of diversity. These Goths keep on pushing their magic formula for reform on us. Nothing changes other than that they are voted into office or hired by school boards who are unaware of their lack of critical thought or their hidden agendas."

"There is a great difference between man and beast, Mr. Pidation," cautioned philosopher Cicero, who had just floated down from the stacks, saturating the room with an accumulation of dust that could be clearly noticed through the incandescent streams of light filling the room. People sitting at both the round and rectangular tables coughed.

"Sorry for the dust," he began. "It comes not from me but from your neglect of me over the eons." Finding a chair and spreading his diaphanous white garment gingerly across it, he took a deep breath, coughed, and began. "People should be cautious when dismissing the power of the human mind.

"'The beast inasmuch as he is motivated solely by his wishes, adjusts himself only to that which is present at the moment, with little thought of the past or the future. Man, on the other hand, is endowed with reason through which he observes events and their consequences. He perceives the causes of things, understands the relation of cause and effect, draws analogies, and connects and combines the present with the future. In this way, he easily visualizes the course of his whole life and prepares what he needs to carry on. Through the same power of reason Nature links man to man, by their participation in speech and in social intercourse'" (Cicero, 1948, pp. 324–325).

"But sometimes the link is weak because people have not been practiced at an early age in the civility and mutuality of social intercourse, Mr. Cicero," Mr. Trey Pidation sighed dolefully. "One has to learn how to do this and the learning has to be evaluated and refined year after year, especially in a democracy. Of course, the Goths do not want thinking people."

The table was silent. It was then that Mr. Pidation turned to Dina. "I called you," the teacher explained, "because I wanted to tell you the truth about our school. During the accreditation process, many of the teachers at Hatchery High School made statements to you that were less than veracious. We repeated the spurious information that the agents of delusion at our school wanted you to hear. I don't feel good about manufacturing the truth but it is mandatory that we repeat someone else's fabrications. The school's leaders demand that we all be on the same page with them, which means we say what we are told to say, undermining our own integrity.

"I don't know if you felt the controlling flavor of the campus during your visit," he affirmed, sucking in his breath. Dina could hear the air escaping through his tensed lips. "It can be overwhelming. Every time teachers go to their mailboxes, they are in fear of the memos they may find demanding their attention, memos that state that if they don't comply immediately with this or that, corrective action will be taken. The leadership here has become more intransigent every day while we become more obsequious.

"The schoolhouse is a nightmare," he bemoaned. "I hate to admit it, but we teachers sit on the sidelines grading student work based upon state models that remove the students' and teachers' capacity for critical thought. And we just watch in real time as it happens!"

"'People ought not to be governed like animals for the pleasure of their riders' (Nichols, 2011, p. 52), Mr. Pidation," political pundit Thomas Paine reflected, invoking the relationship between George III and his American subjects.

"But we do allow them their ride, Mr. Paine," Mr. Pidation railed. "We just don't know how to work against these Goth riders. Because we have no models, we don't know where to start. We school as we have been schooled."

Thomas Paine appeared sullen as he stared into Mr. Pidation's eyes. "'A long habit of not thinking a thing wrong,'" he declared, "'gives it a superficial appearance of being right, and raises at first a formidable outcry in the defense of custom'" (Wilensky, 2007, appendix, paragraph 5).

"For so long we practiced how to control and how to be controlled, Mr. Paine," Mr. Pidation admitted, "that it has become a habit of mind. Few in the schoolhouse question a principal's decision no matter how foolish it appears . . . to her face, that is.

"For my part, the word *mandatory* has been used once too often," he continued. "It is mandatory that you spend at least ten minutes of each period teaching how to take the state test, it is mandatory that you create lessons with certain elements in them, it is mandatory that all teachers be on the same page of the math lesson, it is mandatory that no teacher express his own point of view, it is mandatory that no teacher inject his own view into subject matter, it is mandatory that teachers clock in and out of school.

"My students will one day be adults," he opined. "They won't have any idea about why the rules are there or why they are doing what they are doing. The worst part is that they won't care. They will do and find little reason to question. How can they grow up and participate in a democracy if they have not inculcated at an early age its values, and the skills and behaviors that one needs to live in a democratic culture? How can they cast a ballot when they have not been prepared to know how to discern the difference between a fact and a delusion, accepting sophistry because they are not practiced in critical thought?"

"Yet, Mr. Pidation, we know, those of us who think and reflect and are not of the herd, that public schools are essential to democracy," educators Michael Apple and James Beane echoed in unison. "'We cannot help but be jolted wide awake when discussions about what works in schools and what should be done in schools make no mention of the role of public schools in expanding the democratic way of life'" (Apple & Beane, 1995, p. 4).

"That's because, gentlemen," Mr. Pidation bemoaned, "educators who have adopted a Procrustean approach to change lead us, not apprehending that their tyrannical, one-size-fits-all approach to change creates only negative results for our experiment in democracy. I knew this at one time but then faltered because my critical skills remained underdeveloped. It has taken me a long time to realize this. But I do not want to be controlled. I want to be the man Cicero describes.

"I can no longer take this tyranny in the schoolhouse," he admitted, "where the Goths bully us into doing things that make little sense in the education of our nation's children. We obey their edicts knowing that those edicts prepare the children to become what we have become . . . contrite and submissive. And that is the lesson I wanted to share with you, Principal Macksy. You can take it or leave it."

Principal Dina Macksy chose to take it.

FURTHERING THE DIALOGUE

The state board of education shall:

1. Prescribe a minimum course of study, as defined in section 15-101 and incorporating the academic standards adopted by the state board of education, for the graduation of pupils from high school.
2. Prescribe competency requirements for the graduation of pupils from high school incorporating the academic standards in at least the areas of reading, writing, mathematics, science, and social studies.
3. Develop and adopt competency tests pursuant to section 15-741 for the graduation of pupils from high school in at least the areas of reading, writing, and mathematics and shall establish passing scores for each such test.

The above section comes from a western state's requirements for high school graduation. Think about the Procrustean bed. What are the elements of the Procrustean bed incorporated in these requirements? Will these requirements aid in the preservation of American democracy?

Case Study 1

TEACHERS OUGHT NOT TO BE GOVERNED LIKE ANIMALS FOR THE PLEASURE OF THEIR RIDERS

Teacher Trey Pidation recalls the time when he did not sleep in a Procrustean bed.

"**W**as there a time, Mr. Pidation, when you refused to accept the tactics of the Goths?" Principal Macksy asked the teacher.

"There was," he admitted, resting his chin in a contemplative fashion upon the knuckles of his hand, the arm resting stiffly against the table. "I started out my career as an English teacher, enthused about introducing my high school students to the world of literature. I hoped that, through literature, they would expand their thinking about the world, especially since they lived in an isolated farming community that was surrounded by mountains and cloistered from the urban libraries and cities that were hundreds of miles away.

"By vicariously interweaving their minds with the writings of others, they would climb over those mountains, surmounting the limitations of their environment and thinking. I was their guide and it was my job to move the minds of my students forward and onto new paths.

"It was the seventies," he continued, "and instead of listening to punk rock, I tuned into the issues of social change, even though the war in Vietnam was almost over, the march on Washington had ended, and the crusade for women's issues had slowed. I could see the social climate changing. People were better educated due to the equality movements of the sixties and they felt that schools should be held accountable for the education of students. But in addition, the public also began holding the schools accountable for societal ills.

"And then in what seemed to be the great swoosh across time, a setback in democracy began, pervasively slinking onto the main streets of America. It was as if suddenly hatcheries were springing up across the country, created by small groups of people who hoped to groom children to a particularly insular way of thinking. Waking up one morning to an article in the *Los Angeles Times* about book censorship in the public schools, I found it difficult to conceive that I was living in America.

"The article I read noted that certain school districts across the nation were banning students from reading certain books at school. These books, because they were *vile* and *foul*, could no longer sit on schoolhouse shelves (Taylor, R., 1979).

"I immediately imagined that the students were reading D. H. Lawrence's *Lady Chatterley's Lover* with its explicit salaciousness or Henry Miller's *Tropic of Cancer* with its inclusion of certain expletives not used in polite society.

"Did you object to students reading these books, Mr. Pidation?" Principal Macksy asked.

"I did not, but not because of the reasons I mentioned. I just thought students needed more maturity and a great deal of guidance to understand the themes of these authors. However, I knew that high school students read salacious books away from adult excoriation. I know I did when I was seventeen. How much better it might have been if I had been offered guidance with my surreptitious reading activities.

"As I read further on in the article, I learned that the American Civil Liberties Union had filed a suit against one of the school districts," Mr. Pidation continued. "The ACLU argued that banning books arbitrarily and capriciously violated the students' constitutionally guaranteed rights to a free flow of information. You see, the students previously had been able to read the books that were now being banned."

"But who would deny students free access to knowledge?" Mr. Dewey inquired.

"Certain groups of people thought some books violated their moral beliefs, Mr. Dewey," Mr. Pidation explained. "They were talking about the vile and foul nature of the words and phrases contained in the books. As taxpayers, they argued that parents had a right to choose what children should read and not read."

"If every sectarian group in the United States objected to what students read in school, why have public education?" John Dewey asked contemplatively. "It is the job of schools to guide students through the sectarian thoughts of various groups for mutual understanding of one another. It is the way we grow as a people and transmit knowledge. It appears that these sectarian groups you talk about deny the nutrition that minds need to grow."

"They were at odds with my educational purpose, which was to expose my students to divergent schools of thought," Mr. Pidation said. "Therefore, I imagined that the books people were complaining about were the sort I had read late at night under the bed covers.

"But I was wrong. The banned books were not those of a sacrilegious nature. They included books such as *The Catcher in the Rye* and *One Day in the Life of Ivan Denisovich,* books written with profound poignancy about the human condition. These books were teachers to students. The odd thing was that the people who railed against these books hadn't read the books; they were merely objecting to objectionable words.

"One elderly woman, the article read, counted 785 profanities in one of the books. Another said that in her family that kind of language was not used in her house. People defined books by the number of expletives contained in them. I was baffled!

"In a democracy, we don't ban books or cater to special interest groups. We respect the minority view but don't elevate it to mean that it represents the view of the whole. People were forgetting that democracy was about the will of all the people and actualized by the majority. This country had fought a brutal civil war to keep the idea of democracy alive and suddenly small factions of people were trying to pull us apart again!

"But then one day, my principal, Mr. Martin Net, left a note in my mailbox asking that I see him during my prep period. Since we had already completed our yearly evaluation meeting, I could not imagine what he wanted to see me about. It was certainly not to ask my opinion about education. The meeting was short and he was curt.

"*Superintendent Mac Avelli wants to see you now. Please go directly to his office.*'

'But my evaluation was good,' I exhorted. *'Why would he want to see me?'*

'The books you are using in your English classes have been subject to investigation by him. He wants to see you about this.'

'Investigation? Why would anyone investigate The Grapes of Wrath *or* The Chicano?'

"I was again baffled," Mr. Pidation told the group at the table. "The English Department had taught the former book for years. As a high school student I, too, had been introduced to Steinbeck's great work. And with the other book, *The Chicano*, I followed board policy and asked students to return permission slips because of the profanity in it. One parent objected and I gave the student an alternative assignment although I did not want to because it gives me more work and is antithetical to the reason we are here as educators.

"'How do I move minds forward if one parent objects to what I do?' I said to Principal Martin Net. *'The students are the ones who should determine if they find the books objectionable, sharing their concerns with the class so that those concerns can be aired and discussed. Maybe others would agree with the objections.'*

"But I could tell by the staid glower on my principal's face that he wanted me to leave his office. In defeat, I mumbled that the rules were followed so I could not understand why the superintendent would want to see me. But I knew, after reading more and more articles in the newspaper about book banning, that each year more and more administrators and school boards were yielding to the pressures of small numbers of so-called concerned citizens or parents.

"How can a small group of people dictate what students in my classroom read?" Mr. Pidation asked the group. "I am a public school teacher and it is my job to transmit through practice and modeling the democratic culture of our country and to guide the students' practice as they apply their individual analysis and meanings to the curriculum. My students are entitled to a free flow of information as they collectively share unique points of view. How was I to understand what is happening when these people disrupt that flow?

"Principal Martin Net reminded me that I had to follow the rules just like everybody else and I reminded him that I had. *'Perhaps you should attend the next school board meeting if you are so vehement about this issue. But first, see Superintendent Mac Avelli. He is an affable guy if you do what he says.'"*

"So I proceeded to the office of the superintendent. He was very charming and engaging, shaking my hand with a manly expression of force suggesting perhaps that he was in control of this meeting."

"The agents of delusion," Mr. Bishop interrupted, "'are very sagacious in schooling, and successful in securing fit instruments for their purposes. Delusion prepares his prime agents with charming outsides, engaging manners, powerful address, and inexhaustible argument'" (Bishop, 1801, p. 8). Turning to Mr. Pidation he asked, "Did he use deceit or force to delude you?"

"The latter, Mr. Bishop. I recall leaving his office confused about my vocation as a teacher especially after he inquired if I thought it unconscionable that I teach books knowing that I would be exposing my students to unnecessary profanity and salaciousness. He took the position that the school acts for the parents and it is the school's job to protect the students by sheltering them from inflammatory writing.

"I told him that while I agree that the school sometimes acts in place of the parents, it is also to be understood that this obligation of parent to child is temporary. As the child learns to make decisions for himself, the parent outgrows this obligation. But the child has to learn how to make decisions and that is why we cannot hide knowledge from him. If a child is to think critically, he must have the information upon which to form his conclusions. We are not teaching them profanity or exposing them to salaciousness by exposing them to these books. We are teaching them critical thought. *'Who, but the benighted, would contest this fact?'* I asked him.

"The color of his face turned florid after I said this. He escorted me to the door and I knew I was doomed. We shook hands. His felt clammy. But I was not to be usurped. Students had a right to knowledge and if I was exposing them to values that were in some way wrong, they, the students, had to use their reason and tell me why. Their reason would be the test of my effectiveness, not some misguided parents or administrators kowtowing to minority ignorance."

"The reason the English autocracy favored keeping the people uneducated was because they did not want them to develop the ability to think," Mr. Wood (2011) interrupted. "Thinking is a tool that despots don't want made available to the people. Once people have this tool, they begin to question what they are seeing. That is why those in power prefer their subordinates to be rough, ignorant, and superstitious."

"And the reason why I and many of the founding fathers wanted an educated populace was that we knew this experiment in democracy would fail without it," affirmed Thomas Jefferson.

"Well, gentlemen," said Mr. Trey Pidation, "the superintendent, an educator himself, was telling me . . . demanding . . . that I not educate. It was at that point that I understood why my father and grandfather fought against fascism. It was then that book banning, freedom, and democracy became reality for me. At the school board meeting, I pleaded with the school board to reconsider the superintendent's decision regarding the books he had ordered me to remove from my curriculum."

"Were you not worried that you were going over the head of Superintendent Mac Avelli?" Ms. Ravitch asked, thinking about how punitive administrators could sometimes be.

"My rectitude trumped any fear that might have been kindling within me," Mr. Pidation told her. "This was the schoolhouse, not the corporate world. The thought of retribution never entered my mind.

"At the school board meeting I repeated to the seven board members what I had explained to Principal Martin Net.

"*I didn't agree with that policy that permission slips be sent home for some readings but it was a rule that teachers had to follow and of course, I did. We may never agree with all the rules or laws,*' I reminded them, '*but there are processes in which to change them without doing it unlawfully and in random fashion.*'

"*As you all know,* The Grapes of Wrath *is one of the greatest books ever written and* The Chicano *exposes our Latino students to their culture. A high percentage of our students are Latino, yet, there are few books in the library addressing their culture.*'

"It was while speaking that I suddenly noticed that Superintendent Mac Avelli sat at the head of the long, rectangular table and several of the board members had their backs to me and the audience. I bit my lip as I apprehended the imperious nature of these leaders.

"*John Steinbeck had been awarded the Nobel Prize for the books he wrote,*' I reminded them, increasing the volume of my voice so that the backs facing me would hear me. '*In his acceptance speech, he said that his work celebrated "man's proven capacity for greatness of heart and spirit and for gallantry in defeat, for courage, compassion and love. In the endless war against weakness and despair, these are the bright rally flags of hope and of emulation"""* (Steinbeck, 1961).

"These were men without a vista of thought that you were appealing to, Mr. Pidation," a man sporting a goatee declared, rising from his chair, both hands wrapped around a large gold coin that he had just removed from its red case. "I could almost see them as you spoke, Mr. Pidation," novelist John Steinbeck reported. "They are most probably good men but not educated ones. They don't have the vision to see beyond their own thinking." He sat, pondering his remark, returning the Nobel coin he had received in Stockholm to the red case.

"And my work was praised by both the *Los Angeles* and *New York Times*," rejoiced Richard Vasquez, author of *The Chicano*, who jumped up as Mr. Steinbeck sat back in his chair.

"I talked about your critical work, Mr. Vasquez," Mr. Trey Pidation informed him. "'*Yes, the book contains profanity,*' I told the suits, '*but the profanity is a reflection of the world in which we live. We are not here to teach students that they live in a pristine world without fault or error.*'

"The school board members said little," Mr. Pidation continued, "but one could feel the disquieting atmosphere of the board room, which was replete with townspeople.

"The reason I chose your work, Mr. Vasquez," Mr. Pidation said, addressing the author and elevating his voice because philosophers Aristotle and Socrates were parrying words over in the corner of the library, "was because I wanted my students to read something that did not deracinate their culture. I had gang members in my class and I thought by reading this book with them, they would be rewarded with a sense of their rich cultural heritage."

"It sounds, Mr. Pidation, like you were providing them the experience that I averred was necessary for them to understand knowing," Aristotle said, turning away from Socrates and returning to his seat at the table. "Who could object to that?"

"Come on, Aristotle," bellowed Socrates from the corner of the room. "Look what happened to me when I tried to enlighten my students! The state condemned me. Would you like to have a drink?" He said this wryly, walking toward him, his hand extended, his fingers wrapped around a wooden cup filled with a hemlock-based potion.

Aristotle, his eyes wincing, turned his face away from the drink. "You could have refused the hemlock and remained in Athens, you know."

"One ought never to model wrong behavior," Socrates stated. "I believe that it is always wrong to disobey the state. My act was a disobedience to the state, so I could not escape. I accepted the drink."

"'One should never disobey the school board policies,' Superintendent Avelli said at the meeting," Mr. Pidation told the seminar group. "He believed, as you do, Socrates, that when the citizens elect the school board, they are putting them in charge of their students' education. He said to the audience that he was hired to see that the rules were followed. Those who objected to the board's ruling would be practicing disobedience."

"His argument was valid only if we accept its conclusion," Aristotle offered. "But if the school board and the superintendent have rules to follow, which I believe you call school policy, then who is it that is really being disobedient? You did follow the rules, Mr. Pidation, and allowed the student of the parent who objected to have an alternate assignment. They did not [follow the rules]. They banned certain books in an arbitrary and capricious manner, based upon the demands of a few parents."

"But before I could say anything else, a member of the community stood and, without waiting to be recognized, asked Superintendent Avelli why books were being banned at the school."

"The superintendent explained that he had received a letter from a parent about the books to which I referred and, after he weighed the parent's concern about his daughter being exposed to values which he did not support, concluded that these were not the kind of books to which the town wanted their students to be exposed."

"And then I felt the acrimony inside me rise to a fervent pitch," Mr. Trey Pidation blustered, his face flushing.

"I stood, pointed my finger straight at him, screaming, 'You didn't like a part of the book . . . some words in it . . . so you, Superintendent Avelli, construe the part to mean the whole, throwing away the ability of students to form their own opinions. It is not your job to tell our students or our teachers what to think! It is neither your job nor this school board's job to determine which values are valid and which are not. These books are honest, sincere, and good. Are these the values to which you object?'

"I could see the school board and Superintendent Avelli fidget in their seats. But I was furious and felt a volcanic eruption occurring inside me.

"'*Not only are you not allowing the minds of students to grow,*' I shouted, '*but you have violated my duty to guide them as they practice democracy in my classroom!*'

"I was outraged at the idea that my constitution was being torn to shreds by the Goths," Mr. Pidation explained to the members at the round table. "And then I heard the school board members and the superintendent spew words like *garbage* and *profane*, referring to Mr. Steinbeck's and Mr. Vasquez's works.

"'*These books are not garbage!*' I shouted to the cheers of the towns-people occupying the seats in the room. '*I bet not one of you have read either book. I won't embarrass you by asking which, if any, of you have.*'

"'*Who are you to ban books?*' I asked. '*Who are you to tell students what to think? What are permission slips for? If the parents give their permission, why can't the students read the books? You should all be ashamed of yourselves. . . . You're acting like Fascists. . . . They thought that their values were the only values available to people!*'

"There was applause, I recall, as I spoke. I was in passion mode and never thought, Ms. Ravitch, that I could be jeopardizing my career. This was my country and while America was still undergoing its demo-cratic experiment, it needed critical thinkers to continue it."

"'*How dare you call us Fascist!*' a board member shouted at me.

"'*How dare you ban books in my free country!*' I shot back. I felt my lips trembling.

"A student shot up and didn't wait to be recognized," Mr. Trey Pidation went on. "The student, a Mexican-American, explained in a calming manner that *The Chicano* was about her . . . people with her skin coloring. '*It's not teaching vulgarity. Those dirty words you are objecting to are things in real life. I don't want to live in a fantasy. I want to know the good things and bad things in life. You should listen to us and not bully us with your white values. The color of my skin is not vulgar.*'

"Cheers rang out," Mr. Pidation said. "I watched the school board president's face blanch. I raised my voice, caught up in the momentum of the moments, shouting again, '*These books are not garbage!*'

"Then a member of the public asked the school board president if he had read any of the books.

"*I have not and do not intend to,*' he scowled. '*I don't read that much anyway. And because I don't, I look to the superintendent for answers.*'

"*Why don't we have a book burning as a pre-game activity at the next football game, wearing swastikas on our arms?*' I retorted.

"*You are out of order, Mr. Pidation!*' Superintendent Avelli blared, jumping out of his seat, eyeing me sardonically.

"*No, sir,*' I said. '*The only one out of order is you! To have one person dictate to us his values is undemocratic and what this country fought against two hundred years ago . . . and again in 1941.*'

"*It is the job of the school board members to decide what materials are going to be used in the instructional program in the school,*' Superintendent Avelli snapped, taking a deep breath and sitting again.

"*You represent the citizens of this town and not your personal beliefs,*' I ranted, also sitting down again.

"Then a town pioneer stood up."

"*I quite agree with Mr. Pidation,*' Mrs. Fay Jackson Smith told the school board, leaning her upper body forward as her hands cupped the rounded handle of her cane. '*Granted, the two books in question contain some objectionable material but that has no bearing on the charge that these literary masterpieces are garbage. These books are, in fact, quite the opposite. And, I think, gentlemen, you do not know what you are talking about, not having read the books.*'

"*These books have cultural, artistic, and moral value,*' she continued. '*By reading both these works, students can learn and relate to their own culture and history. My husband was an Okie who lived through the depression.* The Grapes of Wrath *identifies his experience in California. Many of the migrants found homes in this valley during those years. My husband was one of them. Are you gentlemen so afraid to admit that maybe your parents may have been the people who treated them like trash when they attempted to settle here?*'

"*This is outrageous,*' one of the board members shouted, slamming down his fist on the table. '*My family has never treated Okies with disrespect.*'

"'*Oh, yes they did!*' Mrs. Jackson Smith shot back. '*You were not born yet. And apparently you don't know that the term* Okie *is derogatory.*'

"The robot's face turned to dross," Mr. Pidation informed those sitting at the round table. "Then Mr. Taylor, the cashier who worked at the Town Market, stood up and spoke. He was wearing his World War II uniform with two gold bars on each epaulet, indicating his rank as an officer.

"'*If it was only one student who could not read the books,*' he maintained, '*it should not affect the majority of students who received permission from their parents. I support these books wholeheartedly because they are teaching a generation of students about their cultural heritage. When you approach life in narrow terms, you condemn it, limiting meaning to the limitations of your own insights. Is* The Kiss *by Rodin or the* Venus de Milo *too salacious for our young people to gaze upon? Are students not allowed to see bronze* David *by Donatello because the genitals are exposed? Are you gentlemen totally unaware what these great works teach us?*'

"The board and audience squirmed when he said genitals.

"'*To you gentlemen of this school board,*' he continued, '*please look to world history and ask yourselves if you honestly wish to produce a generation of students with limited insights into their own culture. Do you want to be in the company of the famous book banners and burners of the extremist and totalitarian states? I served my country proudly fighting against this. These teachers and students who have the courage to speak up knowing that they jeopardize their careers are not off the mark. You are acting like Fascists.*'

"More townspeople stood up and spoke.

"'*Why not ban the Bible?*' a man asked. '*It is full of sexual references. . . . And why not Shakespeare . . . has the school board ever read about the passion of Romeo and Juliet? And what about Titus Andronicus . . . full of hate, revenge, and mutilation. . . ? Maybe the latter is okay. . . . Violence is okay as long as no offensive language is used. Knowledge is not final. . . . We cannot limit our minds to seeing only what is in front of us. We have to do more than perceive and react. That is what canines do.*'

"Another person stood up holding a Bible. She opened it to a page that had been earmarked and began reading.

"'How beautiful your sandaled feet, prince's daughter! Your graceful legs are like jewels, the work of a craftsman's hands. Your navel is a rounded goblet that never lacks blended wine. Your waist is a mound of wheat encircled by lilies. Your breasts are like two fawns, twins of a gazelle.

"'This reading was from the Song of Solomon in the Bible, 7:1–4 from the new international version of the holy of holiest. The speaker was extolling the beauty of married life.'

"And there were the opinions of those who chose to protect children from contaminated thought," Mr. Pidation told the round table group. A middle-aged woman said this.

"'When it comes to using filthy language in books that are used in the classroom I feel that that is no place for it. I have always felt it was the school's place to build the student, physically, mentally, and morally. If this type of literature is used, the school is defeating its purpose. Books like Steinbeck's are teaching students to live a life of vulgarity and debauchery. I'm with the school board one hundred percent in banning certain types of literature.'

"Days later, what Ms. Ravitch alluded to happened," Mr. Trey Pidation said. "My job was posted. I fought the superintendent's battle to fire me and won but it took its toll on me physically, mentally, and morally. I was drained but I felt I had taught my students by example that we can never allow ourselves to be bullied into believing what someone else tells us to believe. I was proud of this.

"I was glad that I stood up because after this meeting, the townspeople united, formed a committee, and decided to elect new people to the school board. All that took time, but as Superintendent Carl Cohn mentioned earlier, change is a slow, steady, labor-intensive process. The citizens of the town, unlike many educators, chose not to be intimidated by people who tried to take away a student's right to an open mind. And although I did not lose my job, the schoolhouse was replete with fear. It might have been a free country outside the school but when you entered the schoolhouse, democracy was nowhere to be found."

"The fear, I assume," posited Mr. Dewey "occurred as a result of the fact that you stood up for what you believed at the school board meeting. In an autocracy, especially where decisions are arbitrary, as in this case study, this certainly can happen."

"Not if democracy is to be kept alive," offered Mr. Jefferson.

"Educators ought not to be governed like animals for the pleasure of their riders," Mr. Paine remarked.

"But they are," said Mr. Pidation, "unless we as educators stand up for what is right!"

Dialogue 2

HAS DEMOCRATIC LIVING BECOME A HABIT OF MIND?

After a break, many of the speakers at the round table drifted back to their seats after meticulously brushing off with a dust cloth any alien particles or smudges that had settled over the years on the outer surface of their tomes. As they did this, the librarian indefatigably adjusted the seating for the new seminar participants scrambling down from the stacks.

In the intervening time, Mr. Trey Pidation, his shoulders hunched and his head leaning out in front of his body, paid particular attention to the comingled Goths who, after performing motions of bending, flattening, and elongating, suddenly assumed a larger space at the table. Their broad, flat faces seemed to take on features. He suddenly could discern their porcine noses with nostrils that flared in and out, as they sucked in air. Their movements sent spasms of shivers down his spine. "Why can't I make others see them as I do?" he blurted out, his words resonating hopelessly throughout the library.

His impromptu gesture startled Principal Macksy, who suddenly thought she saw something happening at that certain section of the table. It was still quite nebulous and took no form and she didn't quite know what it was she was seeing, but for a moment she thought she felt a presence.

As everyone settled in his or her seat, she once again began the dialogue, explaining to the participants at the round table a first step she took in an attempt to understand the connection between education and democracy. "I had once conducted a very unscientific survey," she began, "where I queried citizens of democratic countries about why our children are sent to school. Not one respondent thought that a purpose of schooling was learning how to live in a free society (Walker & Chirichello, 2011).

"The citizens of democratic countries that I queried," she continued, "were those who meandered daily through the modern-day marketplace of thought, the Internet. People of all ages and persuasions gathered in this venue. It is in this marketplace of thought that they disseminated their bytes and gigabytes of unfiltered, specious information as they idly roamed the streets, using their iPhones and electronic tablets to guide them while twittering monosyllabic bromides to others pursuing similar quotidian lives. Perhaps one day Americans will learn that they need more than electronic devices to function in a free society."

Principal Macksy paused, hearing a pugnacious rasping on the high glass window situated behind the round table. Turning her head and raising her eyes toward the cerulean sky, she saw Plato sitting on a white chiffon cloud, his chin resting upon the clenched palm of his right hand. She followed the trajectory of his eyes. From time to time she noticed he was glancing down over the shoulders of Americans as they electronically exchanged their prosaic knowledge.

"Were you scratching on the window?" she asked him, gazing up at his lean, wan, shoeless feet kicking forward the puffy plumes coming his way. "Why don't you join us at the table?"

"Can't, Principal Macksy," he sighed as he removed his hand from under his chin and straightened his bent back. "Have a class to teach. But as I look down below me at the marketplace of people and examine their daily exchange of information, I see that Mr. Trey Pidation was right to challenge the school board and Superintendent Mac Avelli. The common man still remains rough of mind and is easily duped. He has not taken to heart what Mr. Dewey meant when he noted that democracy is a way of life and it has to be enacted anew in every generation, in every year, in every day, in every hour in the living relations of person to person, in all social forms and institutions. But as I have always taught, only some people are capable of elevation to higher thought" (Ulich, 1947).

Moving the focus of his eyes to Mr. Trey Pidation, he said, "I, too, Mr. Pidation, see that cold, isolated section of the round table which participants are careful to avoid. Though not all see them, many of them feel their presence. Those amorphous forms will become less opaque with time. Unfortunately, when they fully reveal themselves, the American polis will not like what it sees.

"Democracy in the United States is at greater risk than ever before," Plato opined. "There are obscure forces out there that would rather that America more resemble the oligarchies of ancient Athens and Sparta than the democracy inspired by America's Founding Fathers (Kaplan, 1997). Democracy is fragile and cannot be taken for granted. What always is may not always be.

"And it will be at that time when *what was is no longer* that the polis must point fingers at itself," Plato wailed, throwing his hands up in despair "for forgetting the values which bound it together. It is at that time that the polis will understand that it freely handed their power of government over to those who had settled within what Mr. Dewey described as the deep layers of society, waiting for their chance to emerge. Over time, you give them your trust, and over time, they abandon you as you become less than vigilant.

"The citizenry loses vigilance when they are involved in pursuing their own individual needs," Plato anguished, "at the expense of the needs of the whole. They are unaware that in a democracy there is a constant dialectical tension between the individual and the people (O'Hair & Reitzug, 1997) that must be considered before the people jump on a particular bandwagon of thought. Does one serve oneself or does one serve the people? Does one serve the part at the expense of the whole, or does one serve the whole, thereby serving the part? How does one balance the two and maintain the fragile social compact so necessary in a democracy?

"As I observe your world," he lamented, "I see the part that is distancing itself further away from the whole. As I look at the American Republic, what I see is that each person chooses to serve only himself. That will be the failure of your democracy. The machines you carry in your pockets are not educating your students but they do serve to quiet them. Yes, together the machines can incite revolutions, but one must know what to do after the revolution is over.

"I recently inscribed my thoughts on my Facebook page," he said, holding up a magnified view of his page on his iPad 25y so that all the participants at the table could see it. "I wrote all my friends that they are more interested in the prate that their fingers keyed in to their electronic machines than in reasoning the prattle that was scrambled in their minds. My new iPad, with its added telepathic feature, picks up all mind-thought, although there is more empty space than thought.

"My Facebook friends, especially the younger ones," he continued, lowering the tablet and slipping it inside his toga, "demonstrate no interest in the sedulous quest for the true knowledge that will safeguard them against the incipient nature of those sitting in the forbidden zone of your table and who critically analyze, Principal Macksy, everything that is said. Many of your colleagues know that they are there but cower before them as Mr. Pidation does now, and do their bidding as you do, Principal Macksy."

Dina's face transmuted to white as he addressed her. She suddenly felt as if her heart was pumping formaldehyde through her veins. She remained silent, unable to conjure the words that could defend her.

"That's why I left higher-level thinking to the trained few," Plato exclaimed, peering down again at the table. "There are few disinterested men like those two sitting over there, those youngsters Jefferson and Adams . . . men who put the people's interest before their own, using reason to guide their way no matter what aspersions they cast upon each other in the political arena. Those two men, even if they did not always support each other's arguments, were reasonable men who felt accountable for their beliefs (Wood, 1991).

"But for so many," he admonished, "reasoned thought does not appear important. Myriads of citizens do not question why a particular person believes as he does or the implications of the belief for himself and for the common good. As a result of indolent habits of mind, people embrace and subsequently become enslaved by another's sophistry."

Dina felt that Plato was again speaking directly to her. She had silently reasoned the irrational and allowed the irrational to guide her just as Mr. Pidation had. For example, she had publicly supported the state testing programs, knowing that they did little more than waste valuable learning time. She had questioned why she was doing what she knew was wrong, yet had told the teachers they had to teach to the tests at the expense of more thoughtful studies.

"Democracy cannot endure if voters have no idea why they think what they think, other than that someone told them so," the philosopher explained. "There is little investment in knowledge in your schools, Principal Macksy. Your students have opinions but have no skills in investigating the veracity of those opinions and turning them into substantiated verities. You school children but you do not educate them.

"I didn't support your American Revolution, Principal Macksy," Plato admitted, almost as an afterthought. "Along with that historian Thucydides and my disagreeable student Aristotle, we watched and waited. We came to the conclusion that people wanting to rule themselves would eventually turn to anarchy and violence just as they did during that French Revolution (Wood, 2011, p. 190) and once again the Goths, who sit furtively at your table, would rule the day. And maybe they should because they are smarter and more patient."

Journalist and college teacher Charles Saife (2010), who had been listening with rapt attention at the table, interrupted Plato. "It is quite true, Mr. Plato, that in our society there are clever people skilled in using propaganda as a way of undermining democracy. They know how to 'whip up a storm of irrational emotion which results in a thoughtless frenzy' (chapter 8, paragraph 36) by the people who then jump upon the bandwagon with all the other minions, voting against their interests, supporting policies that they would otherwise reject."

"Yes, the Goths are clever at getting people to do what they want," Mr. Trey Pidation concurred. "Theirs is a subtle form of mind control, a mechanism for tricking people into agreeing with their leaders, who only have their own self-interests in mind. It took me a long time to see those Goths sitting here."

"That's because, Mr. Pidation, you are hardwired to believe in reason," Mr. Saife explained.

"Is that why, Mr. Saife, we take the irrational and rationalize it?" Mr. Pidation asked. "Is that why the teachers in the faculty lounge tried to make sense of what they were asking students to do on state tests, knowing that it didn't always make sense?"

"Think about Mr. Cicero's earlier remarks, Mr. Pidation," the author suggested, "as he talked about that which distinguishes a man from a beast. Men need 'a relation to facts, a self-justification to convince them that by acting a certain way, they are obeying reason and proved experience'" (Saife, 2010, chapter 8, paragraph 1).

"Unfortunately, we accept reason without further questioning ourselves as Mr. Plato suggested," he continued. "At this point, we allow ourselves to walk into the trap prepared for us by those who want something from us such as our vote. As a result, we undermine our own democracy. Without questioning, we are robbed of our democratic right to think for ourselves and are fodder for the Goths. Think about the limitations of some minds when books are banned from the schoolhouse, books that have not been read by the people banning them."

"After what you just explained, Mr. Saife," Plato reflected, his eyes narrowing and his face melancholy, "like my teacher Socrates, I wonder if this phenomenal world is worth experiencing. I thought time would open minds but it appears to close them even more."

After Plato concluded speaking, Principal Macksy watched him sweep up the lower portion of his white toga so that it fell over his shoulder and onto his back, reenter his sallow feet into his sandals, and peregrinate to his Leadership Academy at the Ivory Tower School for the Gifted. There his select students awaited his dialectical examination of the erosion of American democracy in the twenty-first century with guest host John Adams, who had just floated away from the table after excusing himself to those around him.

"But the phenomenal world is worth experiencing," announced Plato's preeminent, yet disagreeable student, Aristotle. "I read my teacher's Facebook page," he told the group, referring to Plato's annoyance with the mindless banter of the people of the marketplace. "'It made me sad because all men by nature desire to know. It is wanting to know that separates man from beast. It is knowing why and how we come to a particular idea that is salient to human understanding'" (Miller, 2011).

Aristotle may have been a great thinker but Dina questioned to what extent individuals would question why they thought what they thought. Wasn't it easier to accept another's thought than examine one's own? She had. The school board members had.

You see, reader, the principal believed that the American public could be easily deceived, as elite cadres of people, whose purpose was to promote their personal interests, overran them. She, herself, was a victim of their deception.

She reasoned this after initially supporting the passage of laws regarding the standards and accountability movements in education and then watching as it turned into an accounting strategy, which Ms. Ravitch noted served to punish and reward but added little to the educative process (Ravitch, 2010). Even she was told that if state test scores didn't increase at her school, there would be retribution and, like Mr. Trey Pidation's, her job would be in jeopardy.

The Goths were pushing their own political, economic, social, moral, and religious agenda into the marketplace of acquiescence, in which Dina realized she had for so long been a chartered member. Through such electronic media as the Internet, talk radio, or network television, these agents of delusion spread their sacred words. Sometimes they did it secretly, reluctant to commit their actions to paper (de Tocqueville, 1969; Kaplan, 1997; Sharlet, 2008). And the problem, Dina concluded, was that the polis didn't have the critical skills to reasonably understand what was happening. The polis even seemed oblivious of how to talk to each other anymore, coarseness in language usurping civility.

"What people accept as truth is merely human invention," the American Revolution pundit Abraham Bishop averred. "Mr. Plato might have thought that there was some fixed truth out there but the truth is that what we think comes from us. We create what we believe."

"And that is why we must educate our children to think critically," Principal Macksy enjoined those at the table. "They must be able to interpret and analyze what is being said to them. But will the people ever have the necessary mental resources when their schooling is so lacking in education?" she asked.

"I do not think so," Mr. Trey Pidation murmured, his squinting eyes trained on the Goths. "I know, as many of my colleagues know, that you are there. But we are mostly too exhausted from long days to fight your omnipotence. I did once, but fear exhausts one's energy. Turning students, student performance, and standards into marketable commodities, reducing learning to statistics and numbers, and steadily draining imagination out of the nation's children . . . those are the things we oppose.

"But, I admit, we don't know how to fight you!" He sighed, still watching the Goths, whose eyes, like orbs, began to ignite into glowing embers, widening as they glowered at him. It was at this moment that he thought he heard them singing. *War is a science, With rules to be applied, Which good soldiers appreciate, Recall and recapitulate, Before they go to decimate, The other side* (Schwartz, 1972).

"But I am not one of your soldiers," he said in a muted voice, the energy to fight draining from his body as he sank back into his chair. He could hear the Goths taunting him as they repeated the verse.

"Some of you sitting at this table," advanced American Revolutionary historian Gordon Wood, after skeptically eyeing the portion of the table on which the teacher appeared focused, "fear that America will see its demise if children are not taught how to live democratically. Many of the Founding Fathers had similar fears.

"Mr. Bishop here," he said, turning toward the pundit, "was an important anti-federalist orator who implored the people of the new republic to think critically about the rhetoric of those running for public office. They were mere mortals, he told the people, and they must think about what these mere mortals were really saying to them.

"But people lacked for education," he continued. "The Founding Fathers knew that an uneducated polis would not long stand against the army of the Goths. . . . Here I refer to men like Aaron Burr who were more interested in the gains he could make for himself as president than the gains he could make for the people.

"Some of the signers of the Constitution studied the Roman Empire, tracing the demise of that republic," Mr. Wood said. "Men like Jefferson knew that for a republic to continue it had to be led by men of virtue, men who had no personal agendas to advance, disinterested leaders. They also knew that men were corruptible and structures such as two representative houses and an electoral congress could provide a filter between mob mentality and a functioning government.

"Republics require far more morally from their citizens than autocratic governments require of their subjects," Wood concluded. "Kings hold power as long as they have strong armies and practice patronage and reward" (Wood, 2002).

"That sounds like the schoolhouse," interrupted Principal Macksy. "Leaders reward loyalty, force is pervasive, and those who do not rock the boat are favored.

"Perhaps schools are like republics, very fragile, always having to balance the tensions that develop between the few and the many," Principal Macksy reflected. "But some people might think this sounds like socialism."

"Not really, Principal Macksy," said an English teacher, a Mr. Reed Linkquich, who, interested in the discussion going on, moved his chair from the rectangular table at which he sat to the round table. He then held up the book he was reading. "In this book, *A Tree Grows in Brooklyn*," he explained, "the father, Mr. Nolan, differentiates socialism and democracy for his daughter, Francie, who is confused about what each means. The father agrees that both systems might sound alike and then says this":

> *"It does to me too," said her father as they walked down the streets of Brooklyn in a fine, upscale neighborhood at the turn of the twentieth century. "It is like socialism. In a democracy, each person may not have a hansom but each person has a chance to get it. In socialism everybody, no matter how much money they had, would not be per-mitted to have one. We don't want that kind of government."* (Smith, 1943, p. 192)

"Well, we all know that the schoolhouse is not democratic," Reed Link-quich reflected. "Democracy demands trust. It is not common in our schools and is eroding in our country."

"Well, Mr. Linkquich does make a point," interrupted Roman states-man Cato. "'What is Government, but a trust committed by all, or the most, to one, or a few, who are to attend upon the affairs of all, that every one may, with the more security, attend upon his own? A great and honorable trust; but too seldom honorably executed; those who possess it having it often more at heart to increase their power, than to make it useful; and to be terrible, rather than beneficent'" (Kurland & Lerner, 1987, p. 46).

"And that is why your Rome fell," summarized Mr. Wood. "Those who had power sought to be terrible rather than beneficent. Democra-cies *are* very fragile," he stated.

"You can convince the people of anything and they will believe it," a medley of voices at a certain section of the table cried in unison as their forms comingled, separated, and comingled again. "Tell people lies and they will soon learn to believe them because they don't have the intel-lectual capacity not to."

"Look at them!" said Mr. Trey Pidation. "See how they challenge our dignity. The less educated cannot long survive the vigilance needed for an enduring democracy without education. Less educated citizens are apt to be less democratic and more authoritarian (Elam, 1984). The Goths count on that.

"For more than two decades, studies conducted about American students," he continued, "demonstrated over and over again that al-though students may check the right answer on a paper-and-pencil test about what the Bill of Rights of the Constitution is, they are incapable of defining, analyzing, and evaluating issues based upon those rights. They are incapable of understanding legal or moral issues of the kind raised by controversies over constitutional rights (Elam, 1984). How can students understand their rights if they don't have the mindset in which to evaluate them?"

"And what about students who do not graduate high school?" asked Principal Macksy. "What did the research say, Mr. Pidation, about their understandings of their rights?"

"It found that dropout-prone youth were less democratic and more authoritarian," Mr. Pidation said. "A similar study of youth was conducted decades after the initial ones. It found that a large number of students were uncertain of so many traditional freedoms (Elam, 1984).

"If American high school students could go to the polls today how many of them would vote away some important freedoms guaranteed to all citizens?" Mr. Pidation asked ruefully. "So many of our teenagers are capable of being captured ideologically by the rants of demagoguery, 'favoring concepts as the strong dominating the weak, enhanced police powers, and even sterilization of certain groups of people'" (Elam, 1984, p. 327).

"Would the results have been different," Principal Macksy asked rhetorically, "if students had practiced democracy and the skills of critical thought in the schools instead of just learning about it soporifically from their teachers?

"It is not enough," she continued "merely to school all children. They must also be educated in the practice of democracy. Most students learn about the Constitution and the Bill of Rights four times in their school career (Patrick, 2002) and then take a multiple-choice test to see if they heard what the teacher said. The only way we can be certain that our children understand our democracy is by challenging their minds through application and evaluation of their practice."

"The Goths are cognizant of the way in which the young mind can be manipulated," Mr. Trey Pidation concluded. "It is a worldwide phenomenon to use the innocence of the young mind for one's own purposes. Nazi Germany knew if you wanted to preserve an ideology, you do it through the children."

"I once told a colleague," Mr. Jefferson remarked pensively, "that we are not afraid to follow truth wherever it may lead, nor to tolerate any error so long as reason is left free to combat it. It appears from what you just said, Mr. Pidation, that this is not the case when states deprive their youth of the natural right of thought through misguided school programs which emphasize test scores above meaningful participation and discourse."

"Children are so malleable and they are easily led into servitude," added novelist Uwem Akpan. "In my novel, *Say You're One of Them* (2008), I narrate how children can be duped into believing what adults tell them to believe. As adults prepare the children for slavery, prostitution, or a certain ideological way of thinking, the children do as they are told. After all, their underdeveloped minds tell them that adults want what is in the child's interest."

"Children can be taught to do anything by the Goths and they believe that they are doing it for the right reasons," author David Rosen (2005) admitted. "In the decade of the nineties, prepubescent children in Sierra Leone were taught how to kill by adults under the pretense of democracy. But let child-soldier Tamba Fangeigh tell us the actions he took in the name of rectitude and democracy."

The table guests turned to the youth sitting at the table that had just popped out from the stacks. The boy had soft, almost feminine features. His comely face was strained and he crossed his arms tensely upon his chest as he spoke.

"My name is Tamba Fangeigh," he began diffidently, leading Principal Macksy to ask him to speak louder. "When the war in my country, Sierra Leone began, I was kidnapped from my home by militia forces fighting to take control of the government. I was placed in the Small Boys Unit of the rebel fighters. I became a good soldier doing good for my people even as I cut some people with my machete, killed some, put tires on some, and burnt them alive" (Rosen, 2005, p. 57).

"Children were taught to practice what they were taught," said Mr. Rosen as Tamba returned to his place on the shelves. "Another child told me that he and his schoolmates had met their old teacher and knocked him down. They killed the teacher, burned some of his books and used the pages as toilet paper."

"As I have said over and over again," French philosopher Jacques Rousseau (1964) explained, "children are not born this way. Their actions are due to the adults that school them. These children knew only how to be controlled both in the school and in the bush."

"As you suggested, Mr. Rousseau," added Mr. Trey Pidation, "children can be molded so easily. They can be practiced in anything we teach them."

"They can be trained to be ruthless murderers or skilled test takers on high-stakes tests," he added, "or they can be taught to ask why they are doing what they are asked to do. They can be molded into a habit of quiet acquiescence or they can be taught to challenge the silence."

"But with knowledge, we can be the keepers of our own liberty," Mr. John Dewey stated, his eyes firmly set on the amorphous figures he also saw seated at the table. "I will say it again. 'Democracy is a way of life and we cannot forget that it does not come automatically to us. It has to be *enacted* each day by the people in all social forms and institutions. Unless democratic habits of thought and action are part of the fiber of people, political democracy is insecure. Democracy moves into the bone and blood of people'" (Ratner, 1939, p. 720).

"At one time I questioned," Dina said, "whether the people of the twenty-first century living in democratic countries were cognizant of the connection between schooling and democracy, Mr. Dewey. I began this discussion by telling all of you seated here that I once queried my colleagues and friends in this regard, in order to gauge the proximity of the Goths to completely distilling democracy and defining it in their own terms.

"So I took my query to the people of the marketplace. Why do we send our children to school?" I asked (Walker & Chirichello, 2011). "I received many responses listing reasons, which vaulted from child rearing to the acquisition of skills and knowledge. Missing was the one response that was most imperative to me as an educator. Not one person said that we send our children to school to preserve democracy. This concerned me because I believed as you did, Mr. Dewey, that democracy was a way of life that does not automatically come to us. Were respondents consigning history to oblivion?"

"I believe in the people," Mr. Jefferson remarked, interrupting her thoughts. "But if they lack the skills of critical thought, democracy, which is so fragile, is doomed. Have people fallen into thinking that what they have will always be there? Has this become a habit of mind?"

"A long habit of not thinking a thing wrong gives it a superficial appearance of being right, and raises at first a formidable outcry in the defense of custom," Thomas Paine reminded the seminar group (Nichols, 2011, p. 37).

"Sometimes reinvesting in the ideology behind the habits we have," Principal Macksy stated, "is important in reminding us how we developed the habit in the first place."

The principal concluded from the voices heard at the table that we, the people, had fallen into the habit of thinking that America would always be a free country. The Romans had similar thoughts about their own state. Then the Goths stood at their gates and trampled them—the gates and the people.

Is it easier to do your own thinking, or have someone do it for you? Principal Macksy asked herself. She could not take her mind off the child soldiers of Sierra Leone, especially because she had taught in that country as a Peace Corps Volunteer. Yes, she knew many of them had been drugged into doing their immoral acts (Rosen, 2005). But was it that easy to manipulate a human being?

Had she, an educator, neglected teaching the critical skills necessary to sustain a state that was responsive to the people and guided by the rule of law? Had she, too, forgotten that the acquisition of skills and knowledge, and the practice of those skills and knowledge, provide students with deeper insight in the way in which we view our world?

"Democracy has to be practiced to survive," educators Hopkins (1941) and Lindberg (1954) resounded. "It is a process that children have to learn somewhere."

"But how do we learn what democracy is if it is not practiced in school?" Mr. Trey Pidation queried.

"Maybe," Mr. Reed Linkquich said, "we learn democracy by learning what it is not. I didn't know how to question critically at one time so how could I teach my students? But I did learn by practicing the skills of democracy in another job I had. As a result, I changed my habit of quiet acquiescence in the classroom. Let me explain."

FURTHERING THE DIALOGUE

The following exercise is an example of a state practice reading test administered to high school students by the Arizona Department of

Education (December 10, 2010). Read the letter and respond to the questions that follow it.

2831 N. 6th Place
Phoenix, AZ 85020
January 28, 2009

Dear Mr. Whitman:

I am writing to thank you for allowing Maria and me to use your office as a workspace as well as to compliment your wonderful organizational skills. Maria and I, as you know, have been in your office multiple times in the past few days writing letters to raise money for our community service trip to Pucallpa, Peru, where we will work with impoverished children. Not only did you allow us to use your office space, but also you helped us greatly by providing us with a list of possible contributors. Without your assistance, I don't think we would have been able to raise enough money for such a trip.

We recognize that accommodating our request for office space required flexibility on your part, but because of your exemplary organizational skills and assistance we were able to accomplish our objectives without disrupting your daily routine. Every time we needed office supplies, such as pens, highlighters, envelopes, or paper, we were able to find them with ease. Your donations of the materials and postage needed to send over one hundred letters are most appreciated. We could not have done this without you.

You have helped us greatly this past week. Your generosity will not only provide us with the opportunity to make this trip possible, but will also be a great benefit both to the children in Pucallpa and us. Again, we thank you for your help.

Sincerely,
Amy Fynmore

1. In paragraph 1, what does the word *impoverished* mean?

        a. illiterate
        b. sick
        c. poor
        d. disabled

2. Based on the letter, which of the following statements is an unsupported inference?

    a. The writer will be traveling with someone else.
    b. The writer raised enough money to go to Peru.
    c. The writer sent many letters asking for donations.
    d. The writer is going to Peru for two weeks.

3. What is the position/title of the person to whom this letter is written?

    a. president
    b. secretary
    c. student
    d. manager

4. Based on the text, what logical inference can be made?

    a. Amy and Maria hope to get jobs with the company.
    b. Amy and Maria will receive support from the company in the future.
    c. Amy and Maria will be paid for their work in Peru.
    d. Amy and Maria hope to receive money from other sources.

5. What is the purpose of this letter?

    a. to request information
    b. to express appreciation
    c. to offer assistance
    d. to clarify objectives

Answers are as follows: 1c 2d 3a 4d 5b

The passage and questions above were prepared as one of several practice questions by the Arizona Department of Education for high school students who are required to take the AIMS tests of proficiency in reading skills. Such multiple-choice items require that a student select the best answer from several possible responses. In constructing such tests, it is necessary to develop those questions that best separate the most proficient reader from the least proficient. The format facilitates fast and objective scoring and efficient data collection and summary.

However, resolving the comprehension process to a list of finite skills can be antithetical to democratic dialogue that is generated through exchanges of differing experiences and opinions, recognizing the needs of a diverse population. If the practice session were to actually seek comprehension rather than student ranking and rapid data generation, it should consider a more interactive response than the multiple-choice format. What questions could be added to the letter that would promote dialogue, while admittedly changing the format from the selection of a single best answer to reasoning among alternatives that would still indicate reading skills but would add the possibility of promoting application into action and understanding?

For example, questions in democracy might look like this:

1. Why would Amy and Maria choose to help impoverished children?
2. Would such a project be beneficial to Amy? Why or why not?
3. Who else might you send a letter to regarding this project?
4. What do we know about Amy?
5. Write a letter for one of the wrong answers to this question.

Now, see if you can create your own.

Case Study 2

DEMOCRACY IS A WAY OF LIFE THAT DOES NOT COME AUTOMATICALLY TO US

Teacher Reed Linkquich learns the practice of democracy.

"I don't think I learned democracy by practicing it in schools as a student or a teacher," Mr. Reed Linkquich began, his fingers interlaced as he calmly narrated his story. "In fact, I never thought about the survival of democracy. It was a way of life, a habit of the mind. There was no one out there orchestrating my actions. I was in charge . . . at least that was what I once thought."

"It appears to me, Mr. Linkquich, that you were just another player on the grand stage who never saw beyond the range of your own thinking," Mr. Trey Pidation murmured, not wanting to be heard.

"I did hear what you said, Mr. Pidation, and you are right," he answered softly, not offended by the remark. "I reacted but never put much thought into my reactions. Canines do that. They think only of the now and react to it (Horowitz, 2010). There was certainly a time in my life when I never reflected about my social environment. It was there and I reacted.

"I don't know, Mr. Pidation," he continued, "if I could have shown the prowess you did when you stood up and declared to the school board that they were abridging your rights and those of your students. I was like so many of my teaching colleagues, passive and reticent, not wishing to rock the boat.

"We do not think we have to be vigilant about guarding our democracy because we expect that what we have, we will always have," the teacher said after a moment of quiet reflection. "Perhaps that is why, Principal Macksy, no one in your survey mentioned that the purpose of school was for children to learn how to be democratic. However, since I wasn't cognizant about practicing democratic living in the schoolhouse and lacked perspicacity in relating it to the preservation of democracy, I just accepted what I saw without questioning much of anything. It was not my job to keep democracy alive. That was someone else's job.

"I lived as you did, Mr. Pidation, in a small town, teaching English at the local high school and also had a superintendent named Mac Avelli. In addition, I was a city council official and it was in this capacity that I learned how democracy could be practiced. Up until that point, I viewed the bureaucratic operation of the school and the city council in a similar light. I never viewed either of these bodies in a social context.

"Both legislative bodies are charged with making decisions in the best interests of the jurisdiction for which they are responsible," he said. "The job of an elected official is to establish general objectives and goals, determine major operational policies of the structural organization, and select major leaders, making certain that they are doing the job for which they have been hired (Knezevich, 1975). It was simple. When there was a problem, the legislative bodies solved it by finding out who caused the problem and punishing the person who caused it. It was like running the classroom."

"How did you view running a classroom?" queried Principal Macksy.

"I told the students what to do and they did it. Recalcitrant students went to the principal's office. The classroom constitution was whatever I decided it to be, kind of like the school board that Mr. Pidation addressed. I guess, like that school board, I was being arbitrary and capricious."

"And although I supported you in your request for student disciplinary action," interrupted Principal Connie Sensus, abruptly departing Mr. Linkquich's thought bytes as the librarian scrambled forward with a chair, "I didn't believe in your philosophy of the classroom constitution."

"But you always supported me."

"I did with the hope that you would look inside yourself in order to understand why you supervised your students as you did. You must have noticed that I did not supervise teachers as the superintendent did the district."

"I did and that is why we all liked you," the teacher assured her, "even though some teachers did not know how to deal with it when you asked them their opinion about something. We thought you were the decision maker and weren't doing your job by asking us. But we also felt we could talk to you and you would listen. We never felt that way about the superintendent. He didn't invite people into his office. He summoned them."

Turning back to the full seminar table, he continued his story. "One morning as I opened the door to the teacher's lounge, I felt the unsettling atmosphere that occurs when something unexpected has happened in the school."

"'Principal Connie Sensus was fired at the board meeting last night,' one of my colleagues rued. 'How could this happen without any of us knowing about it? I don't get it. She is the best principal this school has ever had. Avelli is to blame for this!'"

"It was the right thing to do," Superintendent Avelli stated with imperturbable assurance, abruptly appearing and taking the seat next to Principal Sensus, albeit avoiding her piercing glance. "Principal Connie Sensus was insubordinate to me," he said, directing his attention to the participants, "and I felt that she was unable to handle discipline problems at the school. If the principal does not follow orders, the district cannot run efficiently. But teachers should understand this. What do you do with a student who does not follow your instructions?"

After advancing his question, Superintendent Avelli was no longer visible to most who sat at the round table. Mr. Pidation noticed that he had surreptitiously meandered over to the side of the table with the amorphous forms. He seemed to be leaning into them as if he was receiving orders from them.

"The teachers and the students could not understand what being insubordinate to the superintendent had to do with firing a well-respected principal," Mr. Linkquich said, perplexed as to the new location of the superintendent. "I didn't know how the school board members came to these conclusions without the input of the people with whom she worked. If they had asked, the teachers would have all concurred that the principal was fair-minded, worked well with the teachers, and was advancing the academic goals of the school. Because I was not privy to executive session discussions, I can only share with the members of the table as impartially as possible what I observed happening in the small town after the school board announced its decision of nonrenewal of the principal's contract.

"The community became irate, primarily because they were not asked for their input," he explained to the seminar group. "'Principal Connie Sensus was a member of the community,' they explained. 'She had made her home here and communicated with parents.' They contrasted this with the lack of communication with the superintendent.

"Since becoming principal, Principal Sensus kept the people informed of school operations," said a chorus of parents who just morphed in while the librarian, huffing and puffing, scampered about locating and placing additional chairs at the table. As each person found a chair, he or she made individual statements.

"*We thought the charges against her were an excuse to dismiss a woman the superintendent could not get along with.*"

"*Their leadership styles are so different. Mac Avelli demands and Connie Sensus asks.*"

"*She keeps us informed about what is happening at the school.*"

"*The superintendent manipulates the members of the school board, whom we elected.*"

"The parents," Mr. Linkquich continued, "decided to go door to door, informing the people of the town of the school board action and enjoining them to attend the next school board meeting if they were unhappy with the decision. Recall proceedings were hotly debated. However, rationality prevailed and the majority opinion was that the public voice must be heard at the next school board meeting before any further action.

"At that meeting, the room was so full that many people stood in the hallways. Community members spoke of the satisfaction they felt for the job the principal was doing. She worked well with students and they did not feel there was a discipline problem at the school. Could the school board share with the community an explanation for the firing? Could the school board present facts about the discipline problems? If they could not do the latter in public, could they at least reconsider their decision?"

"It was the board's prerogative to make the decisions they did," advanced Superintendent Mac Avelli, returning to the seminar table. "They do not have to give their reasons to the public as this is a personnel matter."

"However, one board member did make a motion to reconsider," Mr. Linkquich said. "The motion failed for lack of a second and the indignant public egressed the board room feeling that they had been ignored. 'The school board represents us, not the superintendent,' they cried. 'They do not represent their personal opinions, but the public consensus!'"

"After that meeting," Mr. Linkquich continued, "I began to think about how decisions are made by people we elect to public office and trust to do the right thing. I wondered how they made their decisions. I wondered if my students ever thought about how I made mine. I began to think deeply about how I made a decision on the council and the importance of the role of dialogue and trust in leadership and democracy."

"It seems that Superintendent Avelli believed that the end justifies the means," Principal Macksy remarked.

"His autocratic management style did permeate fear in the workplace," explained Mr. Linkquich, "especially after the firing. We never did trust him and after he fired the principal, we were all fearful, no person trusting another.

"We forever speculated about what his next move would be," he further explained. "We were no longer concerned about our students, just our job security. Fear escalated when the superintendent placed a memo in teacher mailboxes that reminded them of a school policy that said that teachers were discouraged from speaking to individual school board members."

"But what happened with Principal Connie Sensus?" Principal Macksy asked.

"She remained fired. In the next board election, the people elected new people who asked questions of the superintendent. And I no longer took for granted how people who were given a trust to supervise a body of people made decisions. It was almost as if John Dewey was following me around, reminding me that democracy could not become a habit of mind. The ways and means of associated living had to be reinvented for each generation.

"I learned much from this experience," he reflected. "I applied critical thought to the decisions I made after this as a representative of the people on the city council, especially the time that we, too, had a similar problem with an employee.

"The problem we dealt with on the city council was the removal of the police chief from his office. There were complaints brought to the council by a small segment of the population that many officers were quitting their jobs and accepting positions at an adjacent city. As a result, turnover in the police department was high. Citizens approached the city council outraged that we had let this go on for so long.

> *"The man is not fit for the job!"* a truculent citizen shouted.
> *"The police officers are leaving because the chief is too militaristic!"*
> *"Too many citizens are receiving trivial citations because the officers don't know the citizens and the citizens don't know them."*

"The council, composed of five members, met and discussed in executive session the charges by the citizenry regarding the police chief. We didn't talk about the job the chief was doing. We simply defined the problem issued forth by the protesters.

"'*The problem seems to be,*' declared the mayor, '*that some of the people, a minority, I think, feel that the high turnover rate on the city's police force is due to the way the chief treats his men. So we had better investigate this issue, before it blows out of hand. What questions do we have to answer before getting back to the protestors?*'

"We then went around the table brainstorming the questions as the clerk wrote them down," said Mr. Linkquich.

"*Was the question of turnover real?*"

"*How did our turnover rate compare to the adjacent cities?*"

"*Were the police officers quitting their jobs because of the leadership style of the police chief?*"

"*Were they quitting because of salary inequity with the surrounding towns?*"

"*How did the salary schedule of the other towns compare to ours? Most of the officers who left were hired at a town close by. Why? What did their salary schedule look like?*"

"*What were the turnover rates of other police departments our size?*"

"Why did this town that was close by always accept our officers? Could there be other reasons the police officers were leaving? From where were our officers recruited?"

"As we brainstormed, I began to think that I might have fewer discipline problems in my classes if I had brainstormed the rules of the classroom with my students instead of just giving them my rules for keeping the peace.

"'Well, these are all questions that need answering,' the mayor told the council members. *'So let's set about answering them before we talk to the chief. No use upsetting him if the issue is a nonissue although I am sure by now that he has heard about these people and their charges.'*

"Two weeks later we met again," Mr. Linkquich reported to the seminar group.

"'It appears,' the mayor started out, *'that these officers who left our force resigned as a result of our low salary schedule. Yes, they said when the city clerk talked with them that the police chief was overbearing but . . . well, you tell them yourself, Martha,'* he said, turning to the city clerk who always sat beside him taking notes of the meeting.

"'I asked them about the chief's manner of leadership and they said he was overbearing,' she explained, looking up from her notepad. *'I asked them what that word meant to them.'*

"'They said it meant that he assigned them menial tasks like cleaning out the police car. He also required inspection every morning to be sure they creased their uniforms in the proper manner. But their main reason for resigning was salary. Our salary schedule was among the lowest in the region for towns our size.

"'I also called mayors of the surrounding cities and they agreed that our police department turns out pretty good officers in that they are well trained and disciplined,' the city clerk continued. *'One of them even mentioned that they had tried recruiting our police chief as well as tapping into our officers. I also found out that turnover rates varied in many police departments depending on where the officers came from. If they were local, the rate was low; if not, the rate was high. We all know that there is little opportunity for a social life in our small town.'*

"After this we decided to call in the police chief," Mr. Linkquich related to the seminar group, "because we knew he was feeling the pressure of rumors that run rampant in a small town. He provided us no new information.

"We concluded that the police chief leadership style was militarily oriented. Perhaps this approach was not necessary in a small town, we thought. On the other hand, if his approach was turning them into good officers and if the officers were leaving for reasons other than this, we did not need to consider his leadership style. In addition, we concluded that since most of the officers were young and inexperienced, discipline could save their lives when the time arose. In the past, officers had been killed in our town in the line of duty.

"We also now knew that other towns were actively recruiting from our area but there was nothing illegal about this. But our most salient finding was that our police salary schedule was low. We therefore worked long hours in an attempt to find the money to make it more competitive with other towns in our area.

"As a result of raising salaries, the turnover rate declined," Mr. Link-quich said. "We concluded that part of the problem of high turnover was ours for not keeping abreast of current salaries of police officers."

"What about the demonstrators?" Principal Macksy asked.

"We presented them with the facts. Since they could not dispute them, they left the meeting. They were not happy. They wanted the police chief removed. They had not met the goals on their personal agendas.

"In time, I found myself no longer quiescent about democracy. I pledged that I would never again relinquish the vigilance so necessary to protect democracy from those you call Goths, Mr. Pidation, wanting to overtake it for their own selfish means. I began to think of the way the city council tackled a problem and the way the school board tackled their problem. Even though I didn't know what happened when the school board closed its door on the public, I still believe the principal was fired because the superintendent could not control her as he did the school board. As a result, the school board made their decision and had no strategy about how to evaluate their conclusion."

"'There is no greater evil one can suffer than to hate reasonable discourse,'" Socrates declared, his form supine atop the stacks (Miller, 2011, p. 39).

"When that happens, Mr. Socrates," the English teacher explained, "our experiment in democracy fails. I learned about the process and practice of democracy from this experience and wondered if my students had their own strategies to solve problems in democratic ways so that the Goths would not be able to dominate them.

"While it's true that Principal Connie Sensus lost her job," he concluded, "her fate affected all of us. I, for one, could no longer trust the school board, learning that trust is a cohesive that binds people if they are to live together happily. Many of us also learned not to take these legislative bodies for granted as we had previously. I had never thought about this before and decided that I had to pass it on to my students in some way. If I didn't, they would be robbed of their individual right to think for themselves and might become fodder for the Goths. We must always be careful that our democracy does not become a habit of mind. Each generation must reinvent it."

Dialogue 3

IS DEMOCRACY SOMETHING TEACHERS AND PRINCIPALS DO?

If democracy had become merely a habit of the mind, something that does not come automatically to us, then Dina's qualms about the fall of the American Republic were as real as the Goths Mr. Pidation saw sitting at the seminar table.

"Will the Republic go the way of the ancient Roman state," she asked the seminar group, "or will it continue on its experimental journey, providing the American people with the freedom to which it has become accustomed? It cannot, if the schoolhouse is not preparing students for their role in a democratic world. Instead of focusing on the practice of democracy, I see educators teaching students how to practice not the skills of democracy but the skills of test taking. Will our students know how to approach the level of decision making required of them after the tests are over?"

"They will not," a contemplative John Dewey remarked. "Our society would be more enlightened if each individual practiced the skills of democracy when first entering the schoolhouse. Perhaps then school boards as the ones described by our Mr. Pidation and Mr. Linkquich would be composed of more thoughtfully democratic people."

"Democracy . . . has at its 'basic core, notions of representation, equity, inquiry, reconstruction, and the common good' (O'Hair & Reitzug, 1997, p. 268). Where can a young person experience this but in the classroom?" Principal Macksy queried. "For democratic ideas to come alive, they have to be an integral part of the schoolhouse's social structures and must be practiced every day.

"When I enter a classroom, I usually do not see engaged students," Principal Macksy lamented, reflecting upon her question. "Children at times act out because they are told that they live in a free society yet receive mixed signals when they are held captive for six hours a day in a cell-like venue called school. When they are furloughed from their daily incarceration, they sometimes don't understand why their schooling can't be more like their furlong where children take risks and question freely."

"It appears, Principal Macksy," said Mr. Dewey, "that discipline is placed as a priority, ahead of instruction, because educators have concluded that without discipline there will be no instruction."

"I do think that schooling is *all* about control," Principal Macksy mused. "We separate students because we think we can better contain them. Except for student elections, which I view as a popularity contest, I rarely witness people working together for the common good in the schoolhouse. Recall what Reed Linkquich said happened when Principal Connie Sensus invited teachers into the decision-making process. They were suspicious.

"Today," she continued, "I have invited to our round table friends and acquaintances who answered a question I posed to each of them. I asked them if their teachers practiced democracy in their formative schooling years."

As she read the names of those who had accepted her invitation, she noticed that they all had at least a high school education, attended either public or parochial schools, and grew up in democratic countries.

As the new visitors arrived, the wizened librarian moved in a flurry, dividing them at the table by those who had been schooled in the public schools and those who had been schooled in parochial schools. Dina asked her to do this because she automatically assumed that there would be no democracy in church schools.

After welcoming her new visitors and introducing them to those already seated at the round table, she plunged right into the discussion. "I would like each of you who attended public school to think about whether democracy was practiced in the public schools you attended. I ask this because I feel a great deal of anxiety as I ponder the survival of democracy if it is not practiced in our schools."

Teacher Loraine Johnson peered up from the stack of papers she was grading and said, "I guess we can say democracy was practiced in my K–12 public school because all students were allowed access to a free education."

As Ms. Johnson again turned her attention to the papers she was grading, Dina contemplated the young teacher's response. Access to a free education by all children was what made our country different from many others. As a Peace Corps Volunteer in Africa, she recalled students who looked to education as a way out of their penurious circumstances, at times begging in the streets for their school fees.

But not satisfied by the response, she persisted. "But how was democracy practiced in the schools?" The room was silent as participants reflected.

"Perhaps you need to posit your question differently," Mr. Reed Linkquich suggested. "For many of us, it is a difficult question."

"I can do that," Ms. Lindberg jumped in. "The essence of democracy is the process. The quality of living in a democracy depends upon the quality of the process used in making decisions.

"In a democratic classroom," she continued, "teachers guide students in how to identify their needs and plan together ways in which to meet these needs. They teach children how to work together by *working* together and learning the significance of this process. They learn how to discuss and debate in a civil manner and learn that through group participation; both the individual and the members can grow in critical thinking. Children cannot learn these skills in an autocratic setting. In a democratic classroom, the teacher is the guide, not the ruler."

"It does not mean that students make the rules," cautioned Principal Macksy, "as so many teachers immediately think. It just means that the students learn how to engage in a process where, under the guidance of the teacher, they are learning to work together in making decisions. They are investing themselves in a process of critical thought, debate, negotiation, and compromise in order to provide for the common welfare of the classroom. Isn't democracy about this?"

"Yes it is," agreed American Revolutionary historian Gordon Wood. "'Using this process, a constitution was produced by the Founding Fathers. In order for the constitution to be written and agreed upon by the individual state governments, they had to be galvanized into thinking as a collective unit' (Isaacson, 2003, p. 225). One of the basic issues the Founding Fathers had to think about was whether they were creating a confederacy of sovereign states or a single unified nation. And this took much critical thought, debate, negotiation, and compromise."

"So can any of you sitting here recall the practice of democracy in the schools you attended?" Principal Macksy asked, returning to the salient question.

A smirk passed across medical transcriber Kathy Soren's face. "What democracy?" she said acerbically. "On what planet do you live, Dina?"

"I attended schools in England," began engineer Barry Hunt. His laconic reply was as droll as Ms. Soren's but more illustrative. "Boys! Let's get this straight from day one," he bellowed, imitating his teachers. "I say! You do! This is not a democracy!"

"But if it is not a democracy, then how are children shaped in understanding the skills of associative living that involves thinking, imagining, communicating, interacting, and sharing?" Principal Macksy asked. "How does democracy survive if children are encouraged not to speak to each other while the teacher talks all the time and does all the work?"

"Sorry, Dina," former superintendent of schools John Black said to what was emerging as a common theme. "Associative living! What's that? Democracy was not evident or practiced in the schools I attended. The principal or the teachers made all the decisions and if we questioned their decisions, we were told, 'That's the way it is, so live with it.'"

"It sounds like you and Mr. Hunt attended the same schools, continents apart," Principal Macksy quipped.

A number of teachers had thoughts similar to those of Superintendent John Black. Teacher Noel Brown recalled, "I don't remember school as having any democracy. Counselors and parents guided me to take certain classes like Honors English, but I didn't really have much option but to take those classes."

Teacher Neal Whitehall again confirmed the notion of the schoolhouse as an autocracy. "There was no democracy, Dina. I recall in first grade being apprehensive about reading aloud because the teacher hit us with a twelve-inch ruler if we made a mistake. The teachers and the principals were the authority. Students did as they were told. Misbehavior was punished."

Teacher Michael Hart stated that his early schooling was a blur to him. "In all honesty, I cannot say, Dina, that I experienced democracy in any really meaningful form in the public schools I attended. Teachers taught us the theories of representative democracy, of course, but in practice, I never felt as if I had any voice in the goings-on. A coterie of jocks and upper-crust cool kids ran the student government and I had no contact with any of the issues or decisions involved. I never got the sense that any of my teachers had the slightest interest in my opinions about anything pertaining to my classes or school life."

"That is so true today at my school," Mr. Trey Pidation reflected. "The teachers and the administration are only concerned that the students pass the state tests. The expression of personal views of any depth just takes time away from preparing for the tests."

"Schools were not only autocratic, but they also were punishing," voiced teacher Woodrow Welsh. "Either you performed within the range of norms that were tolerated, or you suffered the consequences.

"I suppose the major lack of a democratizing process," Mr. Welsh lamented, "was manifested in the notion that I can't ever recall being taught why we were learning something beyond *you'll use this later in life*. I suspect that school leadership, from administration to teacher, was very top-down in *those days* and this school culture was reflected in the classroom."

Eighty-eight-year-old retired teacher and principal Ben Thruitall, picking up on the term *in those days*, said that he graduated high school in 1945. "Was democracy practiced when I attended my Bronx school? An emphatic NO," he stressed. "It was an authoritarian system. Teachers were in charge and the students conformed. We sat with our hands folded except when writing. I suppose you could sum up my years at school with *do as you're told and follow the rules*."

"Sounds like what we did in England," Mr. Hunt reiterated.

"I graduated high school more than a half century ago," Principal Thruitall continued, nodding his head in concurrence with Mr. Hunt. "World War II had ended and the horrible discoveries of what the Germans were capable of doing were being brought to light. The world underwent a radical change, and education had to reflect it. I haven't exactly analyzed how this system affected democracy in our country; but it didn't stop the brightest from rising to the top or from distinguishing themselves as leaders who encouraged the opening up of the system."

"But if democracy was practiced in the classrooms of each school," Principal Macksy asked the group, "would the opportunity to rise to the top be available to all instead of just some children? Would less control of students cause more interaction in the classroom and would more interaction produce children not afraid to speak up and express their own informed views? Would discipline infractions abate as a result of more students being involved in meaningful classroom activity?

"In other words," she said, "if the classroom extended an invitation for all students to have a voice, would school be less punishing and, as a result, would more students rise to the top? Mr. Hart thought of himself as an outsider in school. Might he have had second thoughts about his status if the schoolhouse did involve him in a democratic process of education from the first day he set foot in the classroom?"

"The difference between the teacher and the politician," said sociologist Willard Waller (1961) in what appeared to be a non sequitur, "'is in the nature of the public trust which they handle. The politician handles money. The teacher handles children. The politician steals money. The teacher steals personality values' (p. 444). The theft occurs when children are controlled and not taught and encouraged in their thinking, imagining, communicating, interacting, and sharing."

"But I don't think it's as bleak as all that, Mr. Waller. There were ways in which the school did extend invitations for students to have a voice," Principal Macksy reported, "but it appears to me that the invitation mostly applied outside the classroom.

"For example, voting can be cited as an example of democratic practice," she explained, "reflected in the election of class officers, student council, and homecoming king or queen."

"But even that was a joke," computer administrator Don Soren, husband of Kathy Soren, scowled. "Participation in student councils and student courts treated democracy as a means for making rules and settling disputes in isolation of the process.

"From the superintendent down to the janitor," he stated, "all of the officials and employees of the school functioned as operators of the system of divisions and departments that made up the school organization. Although the individual contributions of many teachers were of great significance, this was in spite of the organization rather than as a result of it.

"I feel positive, Mr. Hart," he added, "that you are a good teacher, but as Mr. Waller said, you were early on robbed of that arsenal of creativity and spontaneity with which you first entered the schoolhouse. And that is because the priorities and resulting policies and practices of the schools were limited by the vision and values of the board of education as constrained by state and federal law and the not-to-be-overlooked dictates of tradition and local culture.

"In practice," he declared, "control over budgets and activities were certainly influenced by parents and to a lesser degree the interests expressed by students. And as I noted before, there were of course student government activities, but in reality, student government had virtually no influence on any real issues. When students tried to exert influence over such issues as dress codes, it created fervor, but no realistic outcomes. Students who realized this were at once disillusioned and many opted out of the charade."

"Mr. Soren's statement," said Mr. Trey Pidation, "illuminates many of the finer points of how the aura of democracy can be put on display in the schools."

Undergraduate college student Don Soren Jr. sat beside his father. "Early schooling didn't address much of anything regarding democracy," he began, "except to explain that the United States was democratic. Real explanation of what that meant didn't occur until around fourth or fifth grade when we started learning about history. Most of what I remember was learning about the colonies breaking with England and then we were a democracy. *Democracy* and *freedom* were terms used interchangeably, but I was never clear on their distinctions.

"I also recall slaves being brought to this country as part of the triangle trade or something like that," he continued. "But no book ever said that these slaves were kings, scribes, carpenters, or maybe weavers in their land. They were just slaves without identity, sort of like the doctor's relationship with his patient. My teachers applied no critical thought to what they told us. They merely quoted from the textbook, thereby adding little substance to the less-than-challenging facts.

"It wasn't until junior high," young Soren said pensively, "that I heard about the process by which we became a democracy. The Articles of Confederation were largely glossed over, along with much of the evolution of our democratic state, including the implications of the Civil War and the hundred years following. Most of what was taught was along the lines of everyone *has a right to vote*. In-depth discussion of the subject was largely non-existent until twelfth grade civics and even then, there was no dialogue.

"Overall, I would say that early knowledge of democracy centered on an idealized version of events. There was absolutely nothing of the bureaucracy and limitations of the system until college. There was never any critical discussion."

Many respondents, as Don Soren, Jr., learned about how America became a democracy through arid textbooks, Dina concluded. Principal Ann Gagement, an administrator nearing retirement, curtly summarized the teaching of democracy. "We learned the dictionary definition in elementary school, studied civics in the fifth grade, American history in junior high, and in high school had a government class."

"But hearing the information about democracy hardly teaches we the people the practice of democracy," Dina reflected aloud.

"True," whispered philosophers Zeno, Epicurus, and Socrates in unison. "We not only want to discover our destinations . . . we also have to know the how in how to get there" (Miller, 2011).

"And we especially have to scrutinize the quality of the experience," Dina proffered.

It appears that for Don Soren, Jr. and Principal Ann Gagement, two people who attended school decades apart, the practice of democracy was nothing more than a one-dimensional history lesson devoid of contextual meanings, practice, and understandings.

Democracy is something we do through enactment in the schoolhouse, Dina thought, but rarely are young citizens provided the opportunity to be guided into democratic practices, the school opting instead to do what Mr. Soren suggested it does—pulling students on strings like puppets, something that the Goths relish because it makes their job easier. As he also inferred, students have neither power nor voice, basic requirements needed to underwrite a democratic society. Schooling is limiting in what they can do to have voice and power. But does it have to be? Dina asked herself.

"I did practice democracy in K–12 by the votes we took," teacher Joan Harvey commented. "We elected people to various things, like student council, cheerleaders, and royalty at dances. That's all I can really remember doing that was democratic. But perhaps after hearing what others at the table have voiced, it was not democratic . . . just given the appearance of democracy.

"The voting, the idea that you can control some aspect of society . . . not until college did that really hit me," Ms. Harvey reflected. "It was then that I fully comprehended Rousseau when he said that liberty meant that people had a voice and with that voice could participate in political rhetoric.

"I learned to be democratic," she continued, "by my college experiences as I was immediately confronted by black students while sitting in the student union with a friend. I was asked about Malcolm X, Martin Luther King, Jr., and the Black Panthers, and mocked because I knew very little as a result of my small high school, my didactic history teacher who taught directly from the text, the lack of classroom discussion, and my small town of all white people. I can remember feeling humiliated, turning red in the face from embarrassment, and vowing I would never again be so removed from what was happening in our country.

"I went back to my small town, confronting my history teacher as to how I could possibly be sent to the university with such a dearth of historical knowledge and background of our own country."

"Like the young college student, Don Soren, Ms. Harvey's education was not only devoid of what she considered the essential critical knowledge to understand the diversity of our nation but the practice of democracy was mostly absent from her school, allowing her mind to remain at an equally low level of knowledge," Principal Macksy commented.

"Freedom of thought cannot be achieved," Principal Macksy declared, "if students are handed the textbook version of history and take the quiz at the end of the chapter. They may score well on the test, but without the experience of the content and context of meaning, they have apprehended little and fall prey to the Goths."

"When the schoolhouse actively engages the students in democratic practices," Ms. Lindberg advised, "students become problem solvers and learning becomes an integral ingredient in their experience . . . experience that can be made applicable to other situations."

"Freedom of thought could not be achieved under rigorous adult controls," educator L. Thomas Hopkins affirmed. "Ms. Harvey did not attain this freedom until college. Reed Linkquich did not attain that freedom until serving on the city council. But how many of us don't attend college or get elected to political seats?"

"Students almost always mention extracurricular situations or activity-type classes as a school situation in which they felt most free," psychiatrist William Glasser (1990) stated. "This is where students learn to work together as a group or team, and where they work harder and accomplish more because they help each other and have more fun. But not all students engage in extracurricular activities."

Retired school administrator Vernon Walk expanded this notion of democratic practice in activity-type classes. "I was in debate and journalism," explained Mr. Walk, "and received lots of practice. This included mock congress and student government that was mainly about the proms.

"The senior year of my high school was marked by a series of special studies to meet the requirements of studying the Constitution and alternative forms of government. For this activity, for a period of six weeks, classes were regrouped and the teachers were rotated among them. The head of the department cornered the communist governments, and being a veteran, he taught some of the days in reserve uniform. In the concluding day of the special class a bold student, one who had risen to the rank of cheerleader, raised her hand and asked a direct question of the teacher, whom we called *Colonel*.

"'What are the advantages of such a system?' she asked. 'We have heard nothing of the reason for its emergence. Surely, there must be some benefits of this system or how could it still be around?' The colonel's blood pressure registered in his facial complexion and he invited the student to pursue her question beyond the classroom.

"'If you think it's so great, why don't you move there?'

"There was a general gasp in the class and the student critics were prodded by their fellows to demonstrate the courage of declaration in defense of a student who prior to now was noted for excessive bubble-gum consumption. Sadly, I lacked the courage of a pep rally. However, the topic became a personal concern for us seniors as the Vietnam draft began to thin our ranks in the next several years."

Democratic practice includes teaching students how to work together for the benefit of the individual *and* the group, Dina thought to herself. Many of the respondents dwelt on this point. "Yes, we voted, yes, we negotiated behind the scene . . . and yes, we said nothing when the cheerleader asked an intelligent question and was bullied by the teacher."

Is this the quality of democracy that we want? Dina wondered.

As she heard these thoughts surface to her conscious mind, the librarian quietly approached Principal Macksy. "Do you hear that singing?" she whispered, cupping her gaunt hands around her mouth and Dina's ear.

"I hear it!" she said. The melodious sounds bounded from the location at the round table that was thought both unfilled and filled. "But I can't quite make out the words. Something about war being a science. It doesn't make sense to me."

"They're there," Mr. Pidation bellowed, turning to the principal, "encouraging us to do exactly what we're doing, deluding teachers and principals into keeping schools just as they are. And if you evaluate the classroom you will see what I mean."

Ignoring what she thought she was hearing and discounting Mr. Trey Pidation's cautions, she stated, "Despite what has been said about the lack of democracy in the schoolhouse, there are teachers who strive, through learning and experience, to guide students in the practice of democracy in the schools even as they follow mandated edicts which they know are wrong.

"These are the teachers who have the stuff of heroism, virtue, and moral certainty and will help defeat the Goths just as Mr. Trey Pidation once did and Mr. Reed Linkquich learned to do," Principal Macksy affirmed. "But they too didn't enter the classroom and begin their democratic practice immediately because they didn't have guides in the practice of democracy. As in the case of Mr. Linkquich, democratic practice was applied slowly."

"You are certainly right about that," Principal Ann Gagement, who had been sitting quietly at the table, confirmed. "As a principal, I usually tracked the teachers' path to developing the practice of democracy through seven periods of teaching. Let me share this with you."

FURTHERING THE DIALOGUE

Set up a stack of mental index cards. Arrange them into four categories as follows: roles, topics, locations, and format. Then think of yourself assuming one or each of these roles: a very scholarly student, a very athletic student, a veteran teacher, a guidance counselor, a music teacher, and/or a poor student.

Assuming one or all of these roles imagine yourself debating one of these topics: raising graduation requirements; allocating space in the parking lot for a growing population of students, thus denying teacher space; selecting a new school mascot; including students in the governance of the school; using religious concepts in school athletic events; or eliminating state tests from the school. Argue these topics in one or all of the following locations: school auditorium, classroom, school site council meeting, church, football field, and/or school board room.

Record mentally the procedures you would pursue in dialoguing these issues and the outcomes you might expect, keeping the hectoring *colonel* in mind.

Case Study 3

DEMOCRACY IS PRAGMATIC WITH NO IMPLICIT TEACHING FORMULA

Principal Ann Gagement describes the seven periods of teachers.

"The meaning of democracy has to be started anew with each generation in order to preserve the American Republic," Principal Ann Gagement began. "It is in the evaluation process that I was always able to determine which teachers would guide students through the kind of direction needed for them to become discerning citizens, those who would act independently while caring for the collective whole. A teacher such as this guides her students and has rules of conduct established in the classroom that the students themselves have negotiated and agree to abide by.

"A teacher such as this is responsible to her students," she continued, "just as democratic governments are to the people. When I begin the evaluation process, I can immediately pigeonhole a teacher as to the period of democratic teaching she is in. The earlier the period in the day a teacher is in, the less chance we have to survive as a democratic republic. It is my bellwether for the survival of democracy.

"So allow me to speak without interruption because one of my *stuck* teachers, Ms. Edna Trenched, is about to arrive for her evaluation review.

"When I think about the first period teacher, I conjure up an image of the autocratic ruler of a country who gives little attention to his peoples' needs. In the schoolhouse, I easily spot him. Today he is the fresh-faced young man standing in the front of the classroom, smiling as he greets his Honors English students entering the room.

"This is a young man ready to plant trees and root his first period, didactic presence but he doesn't yet know how to take the gridlike seating chart and see the interactive connections of the young people sitting before him in their rows and columns of seats. He doesn't know the genius of the collective thought that can arise from these students as they debate and gather meaning from within themselves and from within the group. Nothing will grow in his classroom unless he perceives the unreality of his grid.

"It will take this pedant time to understand that students need to feel that they belong in this room, have power here to self-express, and, as a result, have fun. If he wants them to learn from him, he must change their compliant, dormant nature that after twelve years of being schooled will inevitably become their habit of mind. He does not yet understand that education in democracy is a social process of individual and collective engagement in which everyone has a role to play . . . and must play.

"Taking a seat at the back of the room, I notice the neat and orderly desk. Written on the right side of the blackboard is the objective about what the students will be able to do after something is done to them. Written on the left side is the homework assignment, detailing pages and question numbers.

"What will happen in the next forty-five minutes he meticulously writes in his lesson plan that begins with his objective for the students; after reading Johann Wolfgang von Goethe's tragic play, *Faust*, told in two parts, the students will know the meaning of life. I wonder, as I observe him from my place in the rear of the room, whose tragedy it will really be?

"As the students settle into their seats, the first period teacher begins his first period run-on sentence. I hold my breath, hoping that this top group of students will not suffer the slings and arrows of outrageous fortune that I predict will soon follow. For how long will they pretend attentiveness when he renders them powerless? Time will become interminable for them. Can such sentient beings survive this outrage to democracy and the American Republic?

"How can I evaluate him without evaluating him? You might be asking yourself at this point. Experience is the answer. I don't think truth lies in the Forms of Plato but, as Aristotle believed, in perceptible situations that are constantly changing. I make an effort to acquire concrete knowledge about the particulars of what really exists, look for the patterns in what I am discerning which sometimes go here and there and nowhere and everywhere, and draw conclusions from what I see. I also watch as the raw energy and convictions of young people are sucked from them during the next forty-five minutes.

"The fresh-faced tyro announces to his class that today *we* are going to examine the meaning of Goethe's masterpiece *Faust*. When a teacher says *we*, I know immediately that he does not understand the meaning of that particular pronoun in the context in which it should be used.

"He tells the students that the book he has assigned is difficult. Because it is, he will provide an overview of this novel that he describes as an allegory about a man's quest for knowledge at any cost. 'And I will assign extra credit for those of you who can apply this allegory to another universal theme by turning in a paper on something you might have recently seen or read,' he tells them.

"'Universal!' is the enthusiastic outburst from a student sitting in the third row, second seat. 'I just saw the movie *Star Trek*. That's all about the universe and some very Mephistopheles-like people! Can I apply that?'

"A question from an enthusiastic student, I think to myself. This is good because it augurs that maybe I am wrong in my prediction of what will happen in this classroom. But alas, the period one teacher gives an uh-uh and declares something like students should not call out. 'I have said this before and it is one of my most exigent rules,' he declares, rebuffing the student. 'Raising hands is important to preserve order in the classroom. It is a way of learning civility in order to operate in society.' His tone of voice is supercilious.

"The lesson continues. Tic-toc, tic-toc goes the learning up the clock. The assiduous quest for knowledge at any cost continues. I wake up from my somnolent state when I hear his audible voice proclaim, 'So, ladies and gentlemen, that is the allegory of Dr. Faustus.'

"I look at my watch. Forty-one minutes of schooling has become the past. His limbic system is chaotically hurdling synapses as he awaits the laudable press reviews he knows he will receive. He can hear his heart pumping against his chest. His throat is dry; his palms are sweaty. Students take out their cell phones, snap his picture. He has spoken for forty-one minutes and is exhausted, but instead of sitting down, his youthful body sustains him upright.

"Have they learned anything by just sitting and listening to him talk? I did see some students take notes or nod off while others texted messages on their cell phones, concealed under their desks. A young man, a few seats down from mine continues, even now, doing his math homework.

"I doubt they learned much and what they did they will forget by the end of the day. All these students are waiting for now is the propelling moment when the bell will spring them forward. When the teacher asks if the students have any questions, no one raises a hand. The students are just clock-watching waiting to put motion into their paralytic limbs.

"Okay, then, don't forget to copy down your homework assignment," the fresh-faced teacher reminds them. Nobody writes because they have already copied the assignment during the soporific lesson . . . something to do. The bell rings. The students exit, moving into the classroom of the period two teacher.

"'How'd I do, Principal Gagement,' the fresh-faced teacher asks me as I try to surreptitiously escape his classroom. It is difficult to provide an encomium to a teacher who does not know that learning does not happen unless teaching occurs.

"You might again be asking yourself, how do I know that the students haven't learned anything? My experience has always reminded me that when students are taught something in isolation of their engagement in the learning, they feel no interest and thus no utility for the learning. Unless they are somehow involved in it cerebrally, they will resort to their cell phone apps, do their homework, pass notes, nod off, or rebel. As a result of the latter, they wind up in my office and become my problem when neither they nor I originally owned the problem.

"I also know because I review teacher failure rates. When a teacher has high failure rates, it is a signal that something is amiss. So I say pleasantly to the fresh-faced teacher that I will see him after school because I have to be in another classroom.

"But I am distressed and hope that through guidance, he will learn that students need to work in the classroom just as teachers do. The heavy intellectual muscle lifting has to be done by the students under the teacher's guidance. Unless they are given something productive to do, their minds will focus on perhaps less relevant endeavors that serve to fill the emptiness of time.

"I leave, deploring what I have seen. Not all new teachers fall into period one, however. But there are teachers with tenure who have remained there for decades, as is Ms. Edna Trenched, the teacher waiting outside my door. These are the teachers who feel safe doing what they have always done because no one tells them that students don't learn when they are not intellectually stimulated and, when they do tell them, they have no capacity to self-reflect upon what they are hearing. *My teachers taught me in this manner,* they think, *and I am okay. Students have to do their job of learning. I do my job of teaching. It is up to them to do theirs.* These are the teachers who have moved into the quiet acquiescence of teaching.

"Period two teachers experiment with process much of the time after I remind them that students are part of the learning process. Teachers must engage them with useful work in the classroom.

"They tell me that their students are indolent and would rather play with their electronic apps than do any serious studying. Once again, they tell me that it is the students' job to learn and their job to teach. But I know of the unwritten contracts and subliminal messages they transmit to their students: you don't present problems for me and I won't for you. However, sometimes period two teachers change. The change begins when they ask themselves—what is the sense of teaching if my students are not learning?

"It is at this juncture that period two teachers stop blaming the students for not doing their part in the teaching-learning process. They immerse themselves in trying new methods to deliver content other than by lecture. They experiment with such programs as cooperative learning but quickly abandon them when the students are doing other than what was assigned them in their groups. They become so seduced by experimenting with techniques that they begin to sacrifice content. Still when I visit their classes, I see fewer students nodding off.

"For a time, the seduction continues until they themselves realize that content is being sacrificed. In addition, while students are engaged in game playing, the quality of their mental activity is at a low level. When it all fizzles, they grow tired and return to the first period or move on to period three. While the period one teacher is still blaming the students for failing his tests and the second period teacher is looking for new ways of student engagement, the third period teacher is beginning to understand why telling is not teaching and why the cooperative learning process is failing in his classroom.

"The first thing the period three teacher thinks about is why he is in that classroom. Is it merely to tell students about a literary figure some stranger wrote about before they were born or is it his job to guide the students in forming their own conversations with the literary figure in order for them to dialogue with his meanings?

"*They can know what the book is about,* he reminds himself, *but can they combine the themes of the book with their own experiences in order for it to have meaning for them?* What this teacher did in period one is show the students that he knows the profound meanings of life expressed by Goethe and can apply the meanings to his life, but for the students to learn, they must first locate their own identities before they can locate it in others.

"He stops and reflects after everything he does. This is sedulous work. Cooperative learning is a worthy tool for students to arrive at their own meanings, just as techniques like brainstorming, cause-and-effect diagrams, or nominal group techniques can involve all of the students in decision making. But students also have to be taught how to learn cooperatively beginning the first day they enter the schoolhouse. Since this doesn't always happen, it is his job to teach them the skills they will need to meander through the democratic world in which they will live and about which they will be asked to make decisions.

"Period three teachers have flirted with process in period two. Now they are beginning to guide their students in the practice of the interactive skills required of them if they are to think critically as individuals within society.

"I can usually recognize period three teachers immediately because when nobody is around, they are still talking to someone. 'I know students can learn, Harvey,' you hear them say, 'but when will I begin to help my students in developing the right combination of skills to make it happen?'

"Period three teachers do this by taking the great leap forward. They like seeing when the entire class is involved in discussion and everyone is talking at once. They like reading their students' work, replete with judgments about the story underscored by evidence found in the reading. They like seeing what they do in producing a winning result for their students.

"They begin to see that success in the classroom primarily rests upon guiding students in the process of self-management and expression. They begin to see that a self-centered, geocentric, teacher-dominated classroom can paralyze student thinking. They begin to take risks. Students reward them when they demonstrate their willingness to reflect upon *Faust* and its relevance for a seventeen-year-old.

"Sometimes moving out of one's comfort zone is chaotic. But they continue to search for ways in which students will learn to express themselves and engage in decision making underwritten by substance. They have moved from first period telling to the rudiments of third period teaching. They have opened their classroom doors.

"A period four teacher likes looking in the mirror each morning and seeing each of his students as individuals who can think for themselves. He has been teaching them how to do this. As a result, they have learned, through self-reflection and discussion within the group where opinions have been debated and weighed, that students can apply their own meanings to new learning. In fact, period four, male teachers absentmindedly shave twice in the morning and are easily spotted on campus because they have little round Band-Aids on their butchered faces.

"Period four teachers have assertively disciplined, rewarded, and punished; adhered to the Education and the Environment Initiative (EEI); and cooperatively learned. They have thought both critically and creatively. They have gained a confidence in themselves. And certainly after a half-day's passing, they have a right to be right about something. They have finally come to the realization that none of these methods will bring forth from students an ability to think for themselves, formulating decisions developed through critical thought. They realize that education is a social process based upon a critical conversation between people.

"Students can indeed be guided in the principles of democracy in a spirit of open inquiry that is, in itself, an important democratic value. At the same time, students are encouraged to challenge conventional thinking with reasoned arguments and careful research. When students are solving problems important to them which will make a difference in their own living, learning becomes a part of their experience and they can make use of this knowledge in many situations involving themselves and others.

"Period four teachers are launched. They feast, while the other teachers fast. Based upon their trial-and-error tribulations during previous periods, they know what works, what doesn't, when to throw out what, and what to throw out when. During period three they juggled. They are still jugglers, but now they are more confident ones. On some days, they will lecture students on the meaning of existence described in *Faust* within the context of a world that existed hundreds of years ago so that students can vicariously experience the underlying themes of another time and compare it to contemporary living.

"On other days, the students will do the explaining in the context of their own time. Life will parallel literature and it will be lived through the various processes the fourth period teacher has been experimenting with all morning. Sometimes their lessons are not successful; kids are bored, tired of staring . . . anesthetized. But the fourth period teacher is able to know this and self-correct.

"Period four teachers are soldiers fighting for the challenge education offers in the classroom. They are educators by choice, teachers by conviction, credible by experience, hard work, and a willingness to change when their students are no longer thinking. Their morning colleagues may not always be impressed with what they are doing, but the reason their colleagues know what they are doing is that period four teachers have opened their classrooms to them and made available their ideas.

"Period five teachers are very interested in results. The right teaching processes they know will yield the required learning results whether on state-mandated tests or college entry exams. They carry a mental scale in their mind in which they weigh knowledge, pedagogy, and student engagement. They are constantly readjusting the scale in order to create the right balance.

"They are receptive to change and growth because they themselves can always change and grow. They are comfortable with the knowledge that to get the best results from students requires them to open the doors of the students' minds and allow them to exercise their mental perspicacity.

"What's nice about period five teachers is that they are comfortable with themselves. You can spot period five teachers on campus. They're the ones who go around blindfolded, but still know how to find their way.

"Lunch is now over. The teacher's lounge is still at a high pitch of verbal activity. The first period teacher lauds his fine first period performance to the second period teacher who is rambling on about the newest educational technique he has read about which works with students and is sure to change education, as he knows it. Neither hears the other.

"The third period teacher is adjusting his lesson plans on *Faust* after discussion with the fourth period teacher who confidently knows that if he tweaks his own lesson, all the students will be involved in the classroom discussion. And the fifth period teacher is mentally reshaping his earlier thinking about the way in which the students will experience the book because he knows that if he does, student engagement will weigh heavier on his scale, forcing knowledge to rise even further. There is very little science in what teachers do after leaving third period. It is mostly art.

"The sixth period teacher is also about to return to class. Today she ate with some of her students in the cafeteria. Period six teachers are really easy to spot. An incandescent aura outlines their bodies. Their aura makes them very noticeable. All reflective teachers wonder how they can get it because they realize it keeps students awake all period.

"Think of your own sixth period teachers, reader. You may be seventy years old but you always remember the teacher that gave you something extra. That teacher made you feel so important that you really did want to know why Faust was willing to sell his soul. That teacher took you and put you on stage and ever since, when you think of him or her, you are still there, center stage. We always want to know more about period six teachers but they are so busy helping you with you that they have no time for them. There is a mystery about them. What we don't realize, however, is that everything they do, every trick they know comes from teaching the morning and afternoon classes.

"Period seven teachers are the ones you see leaving the campus. You can recognize them because they have that straight-ahead stare in their eyes. It's the twilight period. It's almost dark and time to go home. Teachers in period seven leave the child before the child leaves them. It's closing time and sometimes it is tough deciding when to hand your keys in to the office. Period seven teachers know.

"As we expect students to be enriched and grow from our guidance, we as educators have to continue to do the same. However, the reality is that there are period one teachers . . . and principals . . . who still think that the quiet classroom is where learning best occurs. The more in control the teacher is, the less he will perceive that his students are not learning and the more he will perceive that he is doing his job as a teacher. This thinking will continue in the absence of reflection about the roles of educators in the schoolhouse.

"There is no formula for being a good teacher, because teaching is an art that science can guide, but not control. Once you have learned that we do not live in a mechanical universe where all things are predictable and certain, you will recognize this. You will recognize when a person says, 'I remember that teacher because his affection for his students was evident, and he transmitted it to his students. Rather than fearing the Socratic questioning, we looked forward to it. His questions were penetrating and provocative, but not harsh. He listened attentively and respectfully to his students' responses'" (Pollard, 2013, p. 14).

"And now I must stop because Ms. Edna Trenched, a period one teacher, is still waiting for me."

Dialogue 4

IS DEMOCRATIC LIVING LEARNED THROUGH OSMOSIS?

"**M**r. Reed Linkquich practiced the skills of democracy when he was elected to the city council. As a member of a representative body he participated in group problem-solving activities in order to solve an issue that was potentially explosive," Principal Macksy told the seminar group.

"Mr. Trey Pidation practiced the skills of democracy by addressing the superintendent and the school board who he felt were abridging his rights as well as those of his students over a censorship issue," she continued. "And Principal Ann Gagement traced the skills of democracy by evaluating how her teachers utilized them with their classroom students."

"But what was the quality of my practice?" Mr. Trey Pidation interrupted, seemingly agitated. "For my part, I shouted uncontrollably at the board about the abridgement of our rights as Americans. As I think back, I was not proud of how I presented myself. What a pretentious display that was to my students as they studied my lack of civility and mutuality. All I taught my students was that they had a right to protest. I did not teach them how to do it in a way in which I would be heard."

"And although I did work in a spirit of mutuality and civility with the city council, I did not immediately transfer that spirit into practices of democracy in my classroom," admitted Reed Linkquich. "I just acquiesced to doing things the way I had always done them."

"I too must admit," added Principal Ann Gagement, "that although I monitored my teachers in their attempts at democratic practice in the classroom, I hardly had time to follow up with them. I accepted things as they were because I had little time to do more than one or two observations for each teacher, each year. As a result, I was not able to follow the development of every teacher as they moved from period to period and to aid them in developing their democratic skills further."

"Can we lose our democracy if it is not continually practiced from year to year?" Principal Macksy asked the group. "Can we lose it if principals can't continually monitor the teachers as they advance their skills, or if teachers do not discern the connections with what they practice in one environment with another, or if we are not able to reflect upon the quality of our democratic practice?"

"Can this be the reason why we appear to be becoming a nation intolerant of listening to all views?" Principal Ann Gagement asked.

"What happens when we stop listening to each other?" Principal Macksy mused. "When we don't listen in an understanding and critical way, do we steadily and unknowingly move away from our democratic roots, allowing the Goths to send their minions in and take from us our experiment in self-government? It can't have always been this way."

"Working together and having the skills to work together was a problem even in my day, Principal Macksy," admitted fourth American president, James Madison. "Early on in American history, even before the Constitution was penned, I warned Mr. Jefferson about some of the states that were 'dominated by obscure, middling, narrow minded, and parochial politicians, who could not see beyond their own neighborhoods and responded only to the selfish interests of their constituents instead of the interests of all the people' (Wood, 2006, p. 239).

"Such a state could only lead to anarchy I warned him," continued Mr. Madison, "followed by tyranny. It had happened in Rome, it would happen here. Mr. Linkquich could not see beyond his own neighborhood although I am not suggesting that he is part of the benighted masses. Still, his thinking did not extend beyond the boundaries of the limitations he had applied to this own thinking."

"That is why I thought that a strong national government . . . perhaps an elected monarchy . . . was the only way to unite the states," explained the second president of the United States, John Adams (Wood, 2006). "I knew that republicanism depended on the character of the people.

History had taught me that the public virtue is the only foundation of republics and to have this, people would have to be educated."

"Public virtue, sir?" a flummoxed young Don Soren, Jr. exclaimed, his eyes squinting in the direction of the speaker. Is this really the second president I am addressing? Why hadn't my history classes been as interactive as this? He wondered.

"For a democracy to live, young Soren, the people have to have a natural and social obligation to themselves and others," Mr. Adams expounded. "No republican government could last unless the people believed that they were superior to all private passions" (Wood, 2006).

"You mean we have to care for each other as much as we care for ourselves?" questioned the student.

"Precisely!" said Mr. Adams, pleased with young Soren's understanding. "But I am sorry to say that I, myself, never thought that the people could be taught to submerge their individual desires into a love for the whole. Without that love, democracy could not survive and would be exploited by those lacking virtue" (Wood, 2006).

"Democracy is so fragile," the student mused. "So fragile," he repeated as if trying to make sense of what it takes to preserve it. "Without the Constitution, there would be no United States of America, because as Mr. Wood has written in his many books about the American Revolution, the Articles of Confederation put the will of the states over the will of the nation. It contained no rules that controlled the excesses of democracy described by Mr. Madison earlier.

"My friends think that democracy is about them, not others," he said reflectively. 'I can do anything I want,' they tell themselves. I didn't know what public virtue meant until just now. But I don't think we, the people, care much about each other. We haven't been taught that way. My friends do what they want and would not understand what has been said about democracy as a social process.

"A democracy means that the public good always has to be foremost in our minds," he continued. "I don't think people my age think much about this or its implications for our country."

"That's because we don't practice critical thought in the school-house," Mr. Reed Linkquich said wistfully. "What we do practice is the excesses to which Mr. Madison referred such as children and adults hectored in the schoolhouse. But we don't understand *excess* in a socio-political sense. It is ironic that we experience the factors that can de-

stroy our democracy but because we don't ask what it is in our sociopo-
litical behavior that is allowing this to happen, we can't identify with the
cause of our democratic demise."

"I have seen how the public behaves," young Soren explained, following up on what he had just heard, "when it speaks but does not
listen, when it misuses facts and accepts ad hominem arguments as
truth, when it ignores a fellow citizen lying on the street in anguish.
Have our minds been molded for closure by our own ignorance and the
ignorance of our teachers? Is ignorance transmitted through a conduit
where the older transmit it to the younger? Have we forgotten that Mr.
Dewey reminded us that for democratic thought to survive it has to be
renewed each generation, and as Ms. Lindberg and Mr. Hopkins
voiced, practiced in our schools?

"In America," he continued, "maybe we don't commit the flagrant
acts that the child soldiers in Sierra Leone did, but have we asked
ourselves what events could lead to such a horror? We never discussed
very much about why things happen. If it is not in the textbook, it is not
taught. I wonder if the people sitting here who attended parochial
school had more opportunity at practicing democracy than those of us
who attended public schools. Maybe they are less ignorant than we are
and have more understanding of our social and moral obligations to
others and ourselves. Maybe they understand that the public good
underscores constitutional thought."

"I doubt it," teacher Mildred Savers scowled. "The school I attended
until sixth grade was not democratic in any fashion. We were so frightened that we had no time to think about the public good. Our only
thought was not to get in trouble. A single male teacher ran the parochial school I attended.

"He employed corporal punishment. I felt the swift hand on my
backside on numerous times. When I then moved to public school, it
was the same, only with wooden paddles. Basically the student was
wrong and punishment was meted out swiftly."

Educator Alfie Kohn (1993) elaborated on Ms. Saver's experience.
"Punishment is a way to control, interfering with a child's creativity.
How can a child who fears the classroom possibly be spontaneous or
creative in any positive manner?"

"My teachers at the public school I attended," Principal Macksy
rued, "were so strict that I was afraid to raise my hand for fear of

contributing an incorrect answer. I always thought I was a shy child. In truth, I was a fearful one. My purpose in school was to promulgate the social contract that served the teacher's purposes. I was to be quiet, not heard, and not seen."

"It doesn't make a difference it seems if we talk about public or parochial school," junior college instructor Martha Wendric remarked. "Students were repressed from showing any spontaneity. The way we were treated at my parochial school reminds me today of the way the government treated its people in Nobel Laureate Huerta Mueller's (1994) novel about how governmental repression of its people can suffocate the will to live. That might seem melodramatic but Principal Macksy reminds us of how early in life we can be robbed of our creativity by our teachers, especially those first period ones.

"Regarding your question, Dina, about the practice of democracy in my early schooling," Ms. Wendric proffered, "the obvious answer is no. In high school, we had class officers, but they mostly ran unopposed. It was as if we were receiving in-house training on how to live in Ms. Mueller's tyrannical state. Tyranny in the schools did not prepare us for living in a democratic state. But somehow we learned, or did we?"

"I am not sure we did," teacher Joe Casciato said. "I attended Catholic schools. I doubt any of the faculty ever heard of you," he continued, turning his head toward where Mr. Dewey sat. "If they had, they read your work in order to repudiate your evil teachings. Experimental learning? Experiential learning? Blasphemy! Fear was used as the weapon of choice in which to control us. There was less for them to do when the teachers and principal held the fear button."

"Sound educational experience involves continuity and interaction between the learner and what is learned," Mr. Dewey explained. "Shrouding the schoolhouse in a cloak of apprehension is hardly the way to move the students along the path of democratic participation in society."

Philosophers Hubert Dreyfus and Sean Dorrance Kelly fell from the bookshelves concurrently upon hearing Mr. Dewey speak. "If we are made to lie in Procrustean beds," they said in tandem, "'how are we to find the significant differences among the possible actions in our lives? For it is these differences that provide a basis for making decisions about who we are to be or become' (Dreyfus & Kelly, 2011, p. 12).

'What will I be?' can perhaps be more defining for the child who has been guided in how to think critically."

"Without democracy, our choices are limited," Principal Macksy concluded. "We may dream about what we want to be but because we have been made to lie in Procrustean beds, we have not developed the intellectual capacity to pursue our dreams. How much of our ability to think critically has been unknowingly squashed by control in the schoolhouse?"

"If that capability was blocked by those who didn't want children to think too much," Mr. Trey Pidation said rhetorically, "how do we learn the democratic process in a way that profits both the individual and the collective good of the polis?"

Former school superintendent, college professor, and author Michael Chirichello, who also attended parochial schools, rephrased the question. "If my adventures in the autocratic, almost dictatorial culture of parochial schools began in first grade and continued on until graduation, where did I learn to appreciate and practice democratic ideals?"

"Maybe we learn democracy by osmosis," registered nurse Bonnie Fox suggested.

Everyone at the table turned his or her attention to Ms. Fox. "Maybe it just comes through," she elaborated.

"But what are the nature and the quality of the *coming through* process?" Mr. Pidation queried. "What are the nature and quality of the practice of our engagement skills and the quality of our thought and knowledge? Look at how I conducted myself at the school board meeting.

"Can a poor quality of civility and mutuality," he continued, "lead to the fall of the Republic? If children are not taught the skills of coming together, working together, and critically assessing a situation, will the Goths be left panting at our gates after the necessary recall and recapitulation?"

"If we blithely follow the rules and do not make trouble, we successfully make it through those first twelve grades of school," Principal Ben Thruitall reflected, "but this is not the same as learning the appropriate civility and mutuality to maintain and preserve our democracy. We are not nursed in what is essential to provide the continuity with our democratic experiment in self-government that each generation must practice in order for the concept of democracy to survive."

"Well, we certainly did not knowingly practice democracy in the Catholic school I attended," maintained financial consultant Judith Wright. "Democracy was something that was practiced in government, not in the classroom. You were the student and were expected to do your homework and not speak until you were acknowledged. You raised your hand to speak, listened to the teacher, and did not act up in class. If you followed these rules, your life was good! I do not remember even the thought of democracy. School was autocratic. My job was to learn, the teacher's job was to teach."

"Schools were and still are a dictatorship!" her husband, Jack Wright, a retired Air Force colonel, exclaimed.

Ann Mayer, a massage therapist who attended Canadian schools, recounted the tale of the quiescent student. "I can't say I remember very much about K–12 democracy. I suppose some things were left to a vote and some things we just had to do because the teacher said so. If one conformed to the rules, one would not get in trouble. I don't remember any major feelings of *unjustness* through school. Overall, I think I was treated fairly. I didn't get into a lot of trouble to really test the boundaries either!"

But does conformity lead to other patterns of intellectual behavior anathema to supporting a democracy? Dina reflected. Is this how a quiescent society evolves? Is this how the Goths incipiently meander through the hinterland, chipping away at our constitutional structures, standing upon their bully pulpits and making their way into the substrata of society?

"Once upon a time," Mr. Pidation explained, "during the era of Homeric Greece, the polis thought that the feelings residing in their minds were placed there by the gods. Their sense of gratitude and awe were an external thing. Moods swung, as did the gods. If the gods were happy, the people were happy (Dreyfus & Kelly, 2011).

"In other words, the early Greeks didn't know how to think for themselves," he continued. "It was kind of like the protagonist Winston Smith in George Orwell's (1949) *1984* dystopia. By the end of the book, Big Brother programs Mr. Smith to have only those thoughts that he wants him to have. In the case of the Greeks, the people evolved out of this state of unconsciousness and into a state of consciousness. In the case of Winston Smith, he evolved into a state of unconsciousness and out of the state of consciousness."

Dina asked herself if people today were consigning their state of consciousness in terms of decision-making abilities about the Republic to those who had more time for critical thinking. "This happens," she said aloud, "when we, the people, don't make a mindful habit of democracy and allow others to do our thinking for us, allowing them to take over our conscious minds one byte at a time.

"So one must ask," she said, "if democracy is a group process where people express their own thoughts while listening to the thoughts of others, from where do we learn the process of associative living? If schools are a dictatorship as Colonel Wright and Mr. Hunt averred, does our knowledge of democracy just come about as we do life, looking around us, trying to make sense of what we see? Do we learn by trial and error how to act and how not to act in given societal situations?

"In other words, do we learn the diverse rituals, cultural and social mores of democracy by just picking them up as Ms. Bonnie Fox suggested? And how detrimental is this to our experiment in democracy? On the other hand, maybe some of you did learn the practice of democracy in the schools."

Canadian lay minister Ben Lawdon noted that doing democracy meant learning subliminal social responsibility, "perhaps the *coming through* process to which Ms. Fox referred," he began.

"For my elementary years grades, one to eight, there were many opportunities for us to learn responsibility and assist one another and make decisions. For example, children shared responsibilities in preparing hot meals for lunch, setting up and cleaning up materials involved in art projects, choosing parts for a performance, helping those younger with their school work, taking part in school organizations such as a Red Cross Club, being chosen for a leadership role in both class and out-of-class situations, being the janitor for the day, and being responsible for filling the drinking fountain.

"At the secondary level," he continued, "I attended a school of over one thousand students. We had a student council to which each class elected a representative. This council had the power to direct various student activities and had a voice representing the student body to the staff and on occasion to the school board. One could belong to various other clubs. Each member had a voice in determining the agenda of such a club.

"At the university level, I did not attend full-time and worked as an extension student. I therefore had little voice or power in this situation. I simply had to jump through the hoops as directed. One learned quickly that the majority ruled in making collective choices.

"I view democracy as learning collective social responsibility, as accepting the majority vote, and being a player in the process," Mr. Lawdon concluded.

"But once again," Principal Ann Gagement explained, "democracy was an activity for outside the classroom. Where was the democracy inside the classroom where large groups sit together, engaging in information sharing, and weighing pressing issues interactively? Maybe they don't in Canadian—or American—schools. Perhaps Mrs. Wright had a point when she said that government was something someone else does."

"I also wonder about the nature of the social relationships in terms of civility and mutuality," Principal Macksy remarked. "We all know how hurtful it is not to be picked when the selection process is based upon nothing but popularity. If you were not a player in the process, you had no power or voice. If you were a player, you could beat upon the minority opinion as Mr. Walk explained regarding the treatment of the gum-chewing cheerleader."

"While that may be true," responded teacher Robert Done, "I have to agree with Mr. Lawdon that we did learn, perhaps on a subliminal level, messages about democracy in school."

"Why subliminal?" Principal Macksy heard Ms. Lucille Lindberg mumble.

"The birthdays of George Washington and Abraham Lincoln," Mr. Done recounted, hearing her question, "always meant a bulletin board with pictures and stories about these important presidents. Rarely was there a bulletin board display of Lincoln without the famous phrase like government of the people, by the people, and for the people somewhere in bold letters. Call it subliminal messaging, if you will, but even young minds could not help making a connection that our country was somehow built upon an idea that government was based on the citizens' choices.

"Second and third graders," Mr. Done continued, "obviously have neither the knowledge nor the skill or experience to run a classroom, but my earliest teachers began instilling democratic concepts in our young minds very early. Democracy was practiced, in a limited way, within the classroom."

And like his Canadian neighbor, Mr. Done elaborated about teachers who "encouraged students to pick leaders within small groups to represent them, or to play games as teams during PE. This small lesson of choosing whom we wanted as leaders would then be repeated during recesses, without the guidance of a teacher, as we chose captains for our teams. In terms of picking who would be on our team, there were hurt feelings when certain students were always the last to be chosen."

Would the students feel as hurt, Dina asked herself, if the children had been taught that elections were not synonymous with popularity contests?

One has to also question whether mixed messages about democracy are signaled to the children during these *democratic practices*, Dina thought. The children see the bulletin board that advertises a government for and by the people but see no relationship between what they read and what is occurring in the governance of the classroom. Perhaps only adults join together in making rules, the children may think, but for us, they had to be made because we do not know how to work together. As Mrs. Wright noted earlier, people practiced government in another place.

"Would students be more motivated to learn," Principal Macksy asked, "if they were participants in the rule-making process where they negotiated, bargained, compromised, and cooperated in building a classroom constitution?"

"Please understand that I am claiming neither that we were consciously aware we were learning or practicing democracy," Mr. Done went on to explain, "nor that our teachers were actively using these practices to teach us democracy. My point is that we were exposed to democratic principles incrementally from an early age. Those early experiences would prepare us for an expansion of democratic practices through high school activities such as student councils and voting for our own elected officials in real life later."

But Dina was not convinced. Students could not learn the consensual process of group decision making if the schoolhouse was about control.

Mr. Hopkins, tuning in to Dina's thoughts, added, "In a free society each person has the opportunity to achieve his objectives without the assistance of others but he still must consider the consequences of his actions upon himself and others—the common good. Dewey and I both concurred that democracy means that we are all capable of intelligent self-direction and self-guidance. But of course the classroom teacher should guide students in learning the best means of achieving this."

Dina knew the schools were not doing this. She recalled her own school experience.

FURTHERING THE DIALOGUE

How do you distinguish discipline from control in the schoolhouse? Reflect upon your own formative years of schooling. Is there anything the teachers said about their formative years of schooling that was different from yours? Can students be controlled yet still be guided in democratic practice?

Case Study 4

TEACHERS WHO CREATE CLONES CREATE PRINCIPALS WHO CLONE TEACHERS

Principal Dina Macksy reads from her journals about the cloning process.

"**B**efore sharing my narrative of early public school," explained Principal Dina Macksy, "the one thing I have learned as a principal is that the school setting is fraught with complexity. People have a habit of thinking that because they have been in the schoolhouse, they understand it and have the necessary expertise to solve its problems. The fact is, they have been exposed to a part of schooling and, because of this, know little of the relationship of their part to other parts or to the whole.

"For example, the other day there was another one of those belligerent parents in my office making yet another demand. She entered with the usual lack of civility and mutuality, clucking and strutting in a grandiloquent style her acrimonious message. 'We would not have any discipline problems in this school if the principal,' she spewed, 'would just allow teachers to suspend disruptive students from school. Just let the teachers throw the hooligans out the door!'"

"Well, that is not such a bad idea," Mr. Trey Pidation said blithely, sitting up in his seat, rapt with attention.

"This way of thinking, Mr. Pidation, is why schools are so intractable to change!" Principal Macksy snapped at him, visibly annoyed by his statement. "You hear a suggestion and because it makes sense to your thinking, you immediately want to make it a reality. But have you thought about the implications of such a proposal?" Without waiting for his reply, she continued.

"When I asked the parent to explain what the process would look like whereby the teacher suspends a student, she said that the student would be sent to my office.

"'What if I was not there,' I queried.

'Then he would just wait,' she said.

'And who would supervise him while he is waiting?' I persisted.

'Well, don't you have a secretary?' she scowled.

'Yes, but the secretary is not hired as a detention officer. In addition, a student has due process rights. Is the teacher, with a class filled with students, going to deal with those rights in front of the entire class? What does she do with them while she is suspending the student? And once the student is suspended, where does he go? Someone has to supervise him. Should we hire personnel to do this when we don't have enough money to buy the textbooks we need?'

"The conversation continued," Principal Macksy said, turning her attention to the round table group, "until the parent huffed and puffed away, perhaps realizing that it wasn't so easy for the teacher to take on the job of student suspension."

"I see what you mean," pondered Mr. Pidation. "No wonder I never became a principal. When we make decisions, we have to think about how one thing connects to another. We have to see the big picture. But even that takes so much time away from what we should be doing."

"It wouldn't if you had been practiced on how to see the big picture," Principal Macksy said, still visibly annoyed, "and were a sixth period teacher.

"I have learned that the decisions we make are based upon our prior experiences, which most of us never challenge," Principal Macksy admitted, now in a calmer mood. "We acquire our expertise as we mentally connect little pieces of information that slowly evolve into a *true* picture for us. But instead of asking ourselves about why we are doing what we are doing, it is much easier to just react without putting much thought into our reaction *and* at the expense of building civility and mutuality into our practice. It takes too much time." She said this glaring at Mr. Pidation. "Sometimes what is done to *us* is done by *us*.

"That is why when I make a decision," she continued, "I try thinking about all the people it will affect, the interactions those people will have regarding the decision, the multiple feedback loops the decision will flow through, and the results that will follow, resulting in an entirely new set of processes and assumptions.

"It's less science and more art," she submitted. "I didn't always do this because I didn't always know how to do this. I just gave an order and expected it to be carried out. I was acting more like a foreman in a factory than a leader in a schoolhouse. I conducted myself as my models before me conducted themselves. We learn from each other and most often never question the learning. We are not practiced in doing this."

"Most of us have little understanding of the multitude of processes permeating the schoolhouse," professor emeritus of psychology S. B. Sarason (1990) elucidated. "The links between the schoolhouse structure, the internal and external dynamics, the power relationships, and the underlying values and axioms are not considered because our minds are closed to that consideration."

"That is the way the Goths want it," Mr. Trey Pidation affirmed. "I say, you do. Just the way Mr. Hunt learned it in his schooling.

"It has been my experience," Mr. Pidation continued, "that even those of us who still live in the contemporary world do not understand what makes a school a school and not a factory. For decades, we have squeezed the factory structure into the school building without evaluating its implications."

"The factory structure of the schoolhouse, Mr. Pidation," college professor Lawrence Cremin (1980) explained, "was developed during the nineteenth century because professional educational leaders looked for a model of organization that would take myriads of American children plus the new immigrants and uniformly school them. They viewed the factory model as an organizational construct that could do this. In a factory, with the right specifications, the variation among children could be narrowed so that they all would become patriotic Americans."

"But a factory model of schooling treats children as widgets. Its purpose is to design a schoolhouse to uniformly produce a product with *stamped in America* on it," Mr. Pidation remarked. "Perhaps that is why schools have been so intractable to reform. We continue to be in this thinking mode.

"The schoolhouse cannot change," he said, "until it is recognized that it does not operate on mechanical principles. Instead, it is composed of layers of interactive social structures consisting of irregularities that cannot be always accounted for or forced into place. You cannot hammer a square peg into a round hole."

"Schools are about people," teacher Michael Hart interjected, his hands flailing in exasperation, "not widgets. You can manufacture a desk to specifications, but you cannot do the same to a person unless the Goths produce a Hatchery! An individual has too many behavioral variables. We cannot hope to predict all his individual and group irregularities at any one time! As educators, we have to think outside the box of mechanics!"

"Quite right, Mr. Hart," acknowledged Mr. Pidation. "People relate to themselves, to others, and to the entire school system in irregular ways."

"And these ways cannot be drawn up and shown in a seating chart," Mr. Hart said, thinking about how Principal Gagement described the *first period teacher*. "What we need in school organizations are people who have a depth of understanding of themselves and others. We have to know why we do what we do in order to understand why our students do as they do. In this way, we can make better decisions about the children we are guiding."

"Perhaps we can call these deep understandings 'mental frames,'" said scientist and educator Peter Senge (1990). "These are 'deeply ingrained assumptions, generalizations, or even pictures or images that influence how we understand the world and how we take action. It means turning the mirror inward and learning to unearth our internal pictures of the world, to bring them to the surface and hold them rigorously to scrutiny. It also includes the ability to carry on meaningful conversations that balance inquiry and advocacy, where people expose their own thinking effectively and make that thinking open to the influence of others'" (p. 8).

"I think you are suggesting, Mr. Senge," added Principal Macksy, "that one must know *oneself* to better know the motives of others. People are afraid to do this. There is little trust in the schoolhouse. There is little trust in our society. Look at how little Americans trust their legislators.

"We have to examine deeply why we don't trust," she continued. "For example, a principal aware of the interactive human relationships that exist in her schoolhouse attempts building trust but the teachers reject it, are suspicious. Yet, without trust, how do we continue to live in a democracy? If we don't turn the mirror inward as Mr. Senge advises, the recurrent cycle of control and fear will produce clones for the democratic marketplace followed by the rise of scientific hatcheries.

"Many of you sitting here have recounted your formative years of schooling," Principal Macksy told the group. "As I turn the mirror inward, I see static children sitting in the classroom with hands clasped, afraid to move, sitting away from each other, not permitted to talk, and afraid of their own thoughts. So now, it is my turn to share with you my view on my formative years of schooling in regards to democracy. As Mrs. Wright maintained, democracy was an abstraction that occurred elsewhere.

"I remember reciting the pledge of allegiance every morning in public school but it was just that, a recitation. Nobody ever talked about what the words were supposed to mean or why we were reciting them. When I looked at the photo of our first president, I saw a one-dimensional picture of someone with white hair worn in a style that I did not know existed among men. I knew nothing about the internal man or his motivations in the context of his time. He was a fact in our history book, a widget that once had movement. That's all I knew about him.

"I think also about what Principal Ben Thruitall said about how those who could managed to rise to the top. However, what about the rest of us who also wanted to rise to the top but were emotionally impeded by fear? There was so much fear and distrust in the public schoolhouse I attended. Maybe it was easier to control us but how much did it limit our creativity, our spontaneity, and our ability to grow intellectually?

"While it is true that we did learn some social skills relevant to democracy in school, I wonder about the nature of what we are really learning since the organization does not allow as a primary goal the advancement of social relations, a relevant construct of democracy. Schools have as their responsibility the job of shaping character (Kohn, 1991), but how do they do this when the public clamors against this and we, the educators, do our best to control students?

"I think school did shape my character but it was not in a sharing and caring manner. The subliminal messages I received from my teachers were that I should be seen but not heard. I was scared of the school-house and could hardly wait to graduate high school and be free from its controlling nature.

"When I became a teacher, the first thing I did on the first day I met my students was something one of my junior high teachers had demonstrated to me. Instead of favorably greeting my students, I did as I saw him do. I scowled at the entire class for talking without permission. It was as if I was turning my own fear of school into some rational thought. It worked. They were afraid of me. However, why did I think this was rational? Because it had been done to me.

"In high school, I started a journal. The journal began when I was about to graduate from a large city high school. Let me voice the feel-ings of a seventeen-year-old student about to graduate, so totally en-sconced in fear that she asks no questions in the classroom and then begins to wonder if she will forget how to ask questions at some distant time when she will be required to question. Yes, you will probably find that she was bright but not about to rise to the top in Ben Thruitall's classroom.

"All entries are addressed to a certain Mrs. Newman, perhaps some-one I knew in the past."

Hi Mrs. Newman,

Just want you to know that I will be graduating high school this year . . . but of course, you are already aware of this singular feat. You also know this is just such a good thing because of how antagonizing this cold, stark, and soulless institution called school is. I swirl around in this joyless world, not making connections with most things that I experience in the halls, the lunchroom, and the classrooms.

My father works in a factory and his work reminds me of my work. I do what I am told, never say anything and, after a regulated number of hours, hear a bell. . . . My father says in his factory it's a whistle. . . . I leave, making certain that I have all my assignments written down, while thinking about what's on television this evening.

School to me is like a preconditioning factory where kids like me are prepared by teachers to do the same monotonous thing over and over again as my father does at work: only he gets paid for the number of hours he sits at his machine tightening the bolts on his part of a product that moves past him on a conveyor belt. Sometimes I feel like I am the part on the conveyor belt as I move from classroom to classroom listening to the teachers talk at me. I wonder if all their talk is any good because when I try to put the day's talk together, most of the pieces don't fit and there is no conversation.

Scientifically speaking, school is also like a black hole whose massive density sucks you into it five times a week and smothers you with its sameness until you can no longer breathe. What do you get for succumbing to all that pressure bearing down on your prostrate body?—Paper ensconced in a pool of red liquid!

What is the purpose of school anyway, Mrs. Newman? The adult world says one improves one's lot in life if one is educated. But how can that be when all the school is trying to create is an obedient little mechanical person who will march out into the post–high school world, moving her arms and legs in tandem with all the other mechanical people, just like the bleating sheep in *Animal Farm*, or the obedient workers in the classic silent picture *Metropolis*, or the cogs in the *1984* Orwellian machine. Maybe I am mixing too many movies together and even metaphors, but I spend so many hours of the day in this cold, dreary, and impersonal factory being prepared to be just another member of the mindless flock like in those books and movies.

How do I grow up to be a real thinking person when school is all about memorizing stuff? Oh well . . . at least we don't have to remember what the teacher says will *not* be on the test. But how can so much importance be attached to a test when I forget everything on it as soon as it is over? Is it just to satisfy the teachers' need to feel that they have earned their salary?

You probably know, Mrs. Newman, that since an early age . . . I'd say around twelve . . . I found that I could not always make sense of the barrage of audio sentences the seven periods of teachers run on with. Neuron-to-neuron communication is not always happening with any frequency and so much of the information that vibrates from them to me is lost because of my short-term memory failing to dump the audio sentences into my long-term file. I cannot relate to blah blah speak like the people of the Orwellian world did.

Take geometry, for example. . . . I still cannot understand what all those proofs have to do with anything that is real in life except building a bridge and I have little interest in becoming a bridge builder. Teachers do not tell us about things that make sense like how René

Descartes sat on his bed and watched a fly buzz about the ceiling. It was then he imagined applying a graphical template to the fly's travels and began plotting the x and y of it all.

Now that makes sense in that it tells me something about how all this geometry began in the first place and advanced to a higher level. I can actually relate to the math because it's connected to a real person. My friend, Polly Matt, who knows everything there is to know, told me this story. I am sometimes educated more by my friends than by my teachers. It seems I report to school, but am educated elsewhere. That's ironic; don't you think so, Mrs. Newman?

Have we not learned anything from those who preceded us other than to repeat their mistakes? Teachers have not . . . especially English teachers like Mrs. Kalashnikov, who separates diagramming a sentence from actually writing one. I always fall asleep when the scratching and screeching on the blackboard begins. I just can't sit and not do anything. I do hope, Mrs. Newman, that my exercise in schooling means something. It takes up so much of my day. I can hardly wait to go to college and escape this factory.

Good evening, Mrs. Newman. Today I was diligently studying for my history regents in Honors English when Mrs. Kalashnikov began returning our English compositions, thereby disrupting my memorization of facts about our country's history. Doesn't she know how important these tests are? They influence our entire lives by determining whether we go to college or report to another factory like this one after we graduate.

I felt her furtive glance suck up my whole being as she, like a Nazi storm trooper, stomped her infamous black leather jackboots toward me, slapping the paper down on my desk. Nazis, Mrs. Newman, impress with forceful movements. Then I saw the reason for the searing look. . . . She rat-a-tatted the letter *F* across the page.

Feeling the heat of my body flushing my face, I slumped down slowly into my wooden seat until I reached the point when I knew no one would see my humiliation. I then quickly turned over the paper, coming to the realization that what I really saw was a large and shameful mark from a parallel universe. It was not. I was suddenly in fear that someone would see my very large and shameful wound, which if it became infected, would lead to my demise. I could see it now engraved on my grave marker . . . killed by a big fat *F*.

Mrs. Newman, I have never received a mark below a *B* on anything that I penned. . . . Certainly, this was a mistake of the most egregious nature. Was this an aberrant nightmare I was experiencing? Would the red *F* morph into the more desirable *A* if I stared long enough at the paper?

It was not to be. . . . The *F* bled across the page followed by her comments: "You did not follow the rules for writing a five-paragraph composition. Your paper is also too general." Kalashnikov had bulleted me with her blood-red words. Rat-a-tat. . . . She had killed me for the rest of the period and I could no longer focus on studying for the history regents. My life was ruined and I was condemned to living in a world with mindless, mechanical people who could never again be burnished into intelligent thinking beings no matter how hard they were polished.

I have already explained to you, Mrs. Newman, how I feel about this institution called school. It never does get you high in the sense that you feel good about yourself. It is so insipid and English teachers are so insipid in general. How can creativity follow stupid rules? And what does that word "general" mean anyway? Does it mean that I did not write specifically enough in five paragraphs? Maybe the instructions from Mrs. Kalashnikov were not specific enough.

And specific about what? Maybe if she had been more specific about what was required on the topic of *In Praise to Our High School*, I would not have been so general. But what is there to say about high school other than it is a dull, cold, redundant place to be . . . like all factories . . . engineered in general to keep us in our societal place, void of inspiration that could take us out of this world, and with robot-like teachers who delight in torturing the human mind with bits and pieces of useless information. "Bad teaching comes from the failure to think," I wrote. "When teachers don't think about what they are doing to their students, students don't think about what they are doing to their teachers."

That is most of what I wrote. It was pretty specific to me. I wrote in five paragraphs the reality of my relation to schoolhouse living. I took a risk by being honest . . . and specific. I think I made her mad . . . that is, if she thought about what I wrote.

Hi, Mrs. Newman. In physics class, Mr. Abe Struse was a pleasant respite from another weary, dreary day at the factory. He told us about quantum mechanics and especially wormholes, black holes, and Schrödinger's cat. He said he was not going to have this on the test. I was quite relieved because quantum mechanics is much more difficult to understand than classical physics because even if I memorize all the facts about what I am told in this class, I still don't know how to put them together in order to understand something. But maybe that is the point because this new science deals with uncertainty.

Even Isaac Newton had this problem, so I guess I feel a little better. Polly Matt told me that this great scientist was able to identify the force called gravity, but even he never did discover how it worked. She said that it took several centuries for a man named Mr. Einstein to come along and explain the fabric of the universe. "You see, the universe is so beautiful the way it holds everything in balance," Polly told me. "If the earth would suddenly fall from its orbital path, the rest of the universe would be in deep doo-doo."

Polly Matt says that it proves that nothing lives on its own. Everything is connected to everything in some mysterious way. Everything depends on something else for its existence. I abhor thinking that I depend upon Mrs. Kalashnikov for my existence but the fact is I do!

I often wonder how we can be part of the beautiful universe if we are always locked into school instead. There must be a connection between school and the universe. Polly Matt says the connection exists in a parallel universe. I'm not smart enough to know what she means by that. I got a big fat F from a drone.

As for Schrödinger's cat . . . the cat that represents all possible states of existence . . . it is only when you open the box in which the cat is contained that you discover if the cat is alive or dead. The point of the cat in the box story is that reality does not exist until you pop the quiff wave . . . the quantum wave function where all probable realities are possible. . . . Until then, everything is only a probability. I am not sure what any of this means, but I am glad that Mr. Abe Struse explained it to us . . . and it will not be on the test.

I wanted to ask him questions about what he said, but as usual, I was apprehensive about raising my hand so I asked Polly Matt after class.

Good afternoon, Mrs. Newman. Mrs. Vera Similitude, my history teacher, reviewed questions from past regent exams. I did not have the answers for one or two of the questions she asked us because of the fact that during second period, Mrs. Kalashnikov ruined my concentration as I attempted once again to study. She told me to close the book and pay attention to the grammar lesson. I wanted to tell her that studying for the state history exam at this point in time impacted my life and thus I had a compelling reason to commit to memory the facts of the matter. I had already passed the state English test so in terms of English, there was nothing more for me to learn.

Of course, I said nothing and closed the book until she was out of sight and then reopened it. The last thing I wanted was to have to go to see the assistant principal, Mr. Sid Distic. It is best, Mrs. Newman, to stay far away from this other simian in jackboots.

I always raise my hand in history because I usually know the answers and I like Mrs. Vera Similitude. She's a wrinkled, weather-beaten old woman, probably nearing forty or sixty, but she always positively reinforces me even if I respond incorrectly to a question. She makes me feel good about myself in ways that her metallic counterparts do not.

I wish more teachers were like her, making us feel good about ourselves. When I feel this way, I also feel more confident and readily begin listening to others and questioning. But I don't think the principal of this school feels good about himself so he doesn't make his teachers feel good about themselves.

Mrs. Vera Similitude is probably a rebel and sometimes even asks us different kinds of questions. They are questions where there is no right or wrong answer but she says we have to back up what we are saying with facts. So maybe, Mrs. Newman, there is a reason to use all these facts that I forget right after the test is over. Too bad, Mrs. Vera Similitude doesn't ask more of those questions but she says she doesn't have time for many because of the state tests.

Last week, she asked the class what democracy meant to us. I thought a lot about this question but still don't know the answer. My parents vote for candidates who run for political office. So, I guess democracy means that we vote for our representatives like we do for the candidates running for student council. But the student candidates usually don't say much about what they will do for the student body so I guess that makes them more honest than their adult counterparts who say a lot of things and then are oblivious to the things they said after winning the election.

Democracy should mean our right of free speech. But that's a sham, Mrs. Newman. Watch out if you say the wrong thing in school. That's why my English composition bled so profusely.

Hello, Mrs. Newman. I noticed today that the thin strands of light beams filtering into the bookkeeping classroom bounce directly off Mr. Bo Rish's shiny bald head. I wonder if his head feels heated at times.

The rows and columns of his seating chart are just like the rows and columns of his ledgers and the rows and columns of his probable life. I always know, Mrs. Newman, who he is going to call on because he systematically goes up and down the rows in the same way every period. Mrs. Routin Ized, my first grade teacher, did the same thing during read-aloud reading. This always succeeded in elevating my fear barometer and activating General Amygdala. I could almost feel his almond-shaped face issuing orders through the nerve fibers knocking my rational being out of sense.

Within milliseconds, the hypothalamus began producing a hormone, signaling the pituitary and adrenal glands to flood the bloodstream with more hormones. There was no hunger when the General took over. There was only a feeling of the heart pumping against my breastbone, trying to break through. I felt suddenly wide awake, my olfactory senses besieged by the unpleasant odor emanating from the deluge of sweat pouring down under my armpits.

When Mrs. Routin Ized stood up from her chair and said to her victims, "Okay, boys and girls, take out your readers," my eyes raced to the door, hoping it would magically open and create a vacuum that would suck me into it and out to a parallel universe where fear does not exist. Unable to do that, I began counting the number of kids who would read before me, calculating my turn, and the paragraph I would be reading. Then if I did not know a word in that particular paragraph, I would whisper to Polly Matt, who sat next to me . . . how do you say so-and-so . . . and I would clandestinely point to the word. This whole process of read-aloud reading made *Dick and Jane* not very much fun.

I really feared, Mrs. Newman, being unable to decipher a word because of the Routin Ized phonics torture method, a favorite tool of jackbooters. She had the deficient readers struggle through each consonant and vowel until they were able to string the sounds together and produce an intelligible-sounding word.

Sometimes you just cannot scare the right word out of a frightened kid. Kids know that . . . why don't teachers? Didn't they take biology and know about the General?

Mrs. Kalashnikov was just like Mrs. Routin Ized. They both seemed to be emboldened by beating us mentally black and blue in front of an audience. I think it made them feel as if they were stronger people . . . like female Hitlers who, for periods at a time, controlled you in their concentration class.

Good evening, Mrs. Newman. It was not a good day at the factory! In Honors English today, Mrs. Kalashnikov rat-a-tatted me again because of my inability to show her that I had indeed memorized the first stanza of "Sea Fever" by John Masefield. When she began scanning the terrain, looking for new victims to demonstrate her control of their fate, I froze, praying that I was not within her gun barrel's sight. General Amygdala was working overtime within the confines of my body.

Ra-ta-ta-ta. Her gunfire sprayed bullets across the room, students ducking under their desks, but I was too late. Her bullets found their target.

"Dina, it is your turn," she announced. The bullets had popped the quiff. The cat had died. I was no longer in another universe. The General had taken charge of my being. I was trapped in his fear.

Feebly, I began the recitation, praying the words would be there, in the right order. Please, God, I thought, if ever there was a time to experience *YOU*, it is now!

"I must go down to the sea again," I managed to get out, "to the lonely sea and sky . . . and all I ask is a tall ship and a star to stare her by . . . and the wheel's kick and . . ." I stopped. I stammered. I blurted out sounds but they were not forming sensible words. The neural transmissions were not connecting. Everybody was staring at me. I hoped Mom had taken the stain out of the white blouse . . . a hand-me-down from my sister Ruth that I was wearing . . . "and the flung spray and the blown spume, and the sea-gulls . . . and the sea-gulls . . . and the sea-gulls" . . . and then the laughter all around me.

The quiff went pop again, and my body, pummeled by gunfire and giggles, expired. The grave marker would read rat-a-tatted by enemy fire.

I recited the poem all of last night and all of this morning before school with perfection because I loved the words and the thoughts that swept me away to another parallel universe as I recited them. But, Mrs. Newman, I could not do it in the classroom with all those people staring at me. I could not do it because I was afraid that I would make a mistake.

Then the war games turned bloodier. . . . I waited for her to dispatch another round from her weapon and she did not disappoint.

She held her right arm straight out, the index finger pointing directly at my shattered body.

"You should have studied harder!" she said, her countenance transmuting into the three faces of Cerberus. I was now crossing the River Styx, Mrs. Newman, to the staccato sounds from three voices shouting in unison. "You . . . Should . . . Have . . . Studied . . . Harder. This was not a difficult assignment! If you do not work hard and study, you will never get anywhere. You will wind up working in a factory. Now sit down and we'll hear from those who did do their homework . . . those who will be something. Those who will rise to the top!"

I too wanted to be something and rise to the top, I thought as I retreated into a parallel universe on the ocean and swore that I would never become a teacher, Mrs. Newman. How does being a prize of life transmute into a machine-gunning dross like ruthless Mrs. Kalashnikov?

I do believe, Mrs. Newman, that most of my teachers read only books by the Marquis de Sade. They really do believe that doing harm to others . . . no matter how perverted and no matter what the consequences . . . is one of the chief tenets of teaching.

But, on the other hand, Mrs. Newman, Mrs. Kalashnikov, deep down, is trying to make me a better person so I need to study harder if I am to be a worthy person in life. But why can't the teachers in school know that there are students who fear being there?

A Good Evening, Mrs. Newman. A great day today is! Having passed all the state and school requirements, I graduated high school. In the afternoon, I bought a college sweatshirt that told every person in the world that I was a college student although I am not certain that a person who knows only facts but has trouble connecting them should go to college. Still, I am on my way to a new life, a freer one, but I am still not certain what democracy really is. And if I am not certain, how will I know if I have become just another robotic being?

After school, Mom gave me a letter addressed to me from the electric company Con Edison . . . you remember, Mrs. Newman . . . where my sister Ruth works. The writer of the letter, a Miss T. Nottingham, sent me "sincere congratulations on my graduation from high school" and asked if I was interested in training as a stenographer or typist after I graduate. "Con Edison offers an excellent training program with planned advancement opportunities," she wrote. "Why don't you stop by after school hours and visit us?"

Ruth encouraged me, saying that it was a good job for a woman, paid well, and in addition, I could meet guys there. I knew instantly that it was an Orwellian trap.

Dialogue 5

IS YOUR PHILOSOPHY OF PEOPLE MORE RELEVANT THAN YOUR PHILOSOPHY OF EDUCATION?

"**Y**our narrative suggests to me, Principal Macksy," William Glasser stated, "that an education which has the student ask what she is supposed to do, and what will happen to her if she does not do it, is an education based upon punishment and control; it certainly lacks in democratic underpinnings. It is more of a power struggle about who has the upper hand."

"Mrs. Kalashnikov was a controlling teacher, Principal Macksy," Reed Linkquich added. "Young minds are malleable and capable of being influenced so easily by adults. We have heard from Tamba Fangeigh, the child soldier of Sierra Leone, about the crimes committed by children under the guise of rectitude. Without knowledge, they will submit to the adult as you finally did.

"You allowed her the upper hand," he continued, "because you had neither the knowledge nor the guides that could lead you through your own thinking. Of course, the history teacher attempted to draw you out, but she was too busy preparing you for the state test to make further inroads into guiding students into developing critical thought. School had molded you into an obedient clone, just like your teachers had been."

"*War is a science, with rules to be applied, which good soldiers appreciate, recall, and recapitulate, before they go to decimate, the oth-*

er side" a chorus of hazy figures at the end of the table was thought by some to be chanting. "Here's one for us!" they snarled.

"But you loved the words in Masefield's poem," Principal Ben Thruitall pointed out, his eyes squinting as he turned toward the sound he thought he might have heard. "They took you vicariously to the sea. All Mrs. Kalashnikov wanted to know was that you had memorized the poem to her satisfaction. She did not explore other ways of processing the student's knowledge of the poem because she was a first period teacher."

"She didn't grow and she kept her students from growing," Principal Macksy lamented. "Yet some of us still felt she was in the right and we were in the wrong for not doing what she demanded of us.

"Control has such a force behind it, doesn't it?" Principal Macksy commented rhetorically. "It inhibits our thought, our creativity and spontaneity. Like Ms. Harvey, I didn't realize until college the limitations I placed on my own thinking. I had no confidence in what I thought or said and usually was apprehensive about expressing an opinion for fear of being wrong. In addition, I didn't know how to defend what I said if someone refuted me. I didn't know what the right answer was.

"As a teacher, I encouraged my students to think critically in order to build their confidence. But I recall them telling me that thinking is hard because few of their other teachers required them to do it. I know what they mean when they say thinking is hard. Few had encouraged me to do this.

"As a young teacher," Principal Macksy continued, "even though I was aware that I did not want to teach as my teachers taught, I was still so ingrained with a mindset that said children are to be seen and not heard in the classroom that I taught as my teachers did. My classrooms were quiet, orderly, and students regurgitated what I told them or what they read in their textbooks. My evaluations were excellent.

"We tell ourselves that we will not do as our teachers did to us," she averred, "but lacking other models, we do it anyway; we learn from those around us and feel safe acting within those boundaries. As a result, we never question the learning.

"When I began teaching," she said, "I knew that I had to be in charge of the classroom. I was teaching in Sierra Leone, an African nation that had just gained its independence. I felt it was my job to inculcate my students with the practice of democracy so that they could see what it looked like and prepare them for their democratic roles in their country. But I wasn't certain about how to do this.

"I thought of the provocative questions that Mrs. Vera Similitude had asked but found that my students couldn't answer them. They had quizzical looks on their faces when I asked a question that didn't require a rote response. So, I retreated to Mrs. Kalashnikov's classroom where the boundaries were already set. I assumed a didactic posture just as the first period teacher does.

"Then I thought maybe I should go outside the classroom and locate democratic practice in the schoolhouse itself. Maybe the model for what my classroom should look like was the same model that the principal used to manage the schoolhouse. But one day I attended my first faculty meeting and I found that models for democratic practice were not to be found with the schoolhouse leaders. More on that meeting will come later.

"A decade later, as a tyro principal, each time I passed a classroom that was noisy, I cast a baleful glare at the teacher. I then called her into my office, demanding to see her classroom discipline plan, something that I required all of my teachers to write and follow. As long as students were quiet, they were learning, I assumed. At least that is what I used to think. I never thought about the entire learning process, just the part that I thought was broken and that was usually the discipline one. It was my job to tell the teacher to fix it."

"Many principals view teachers as subordinates in need of control just as you did," remarked Alfie Kohn.

"And most teachers view students in the same manner," William Glasser added.

"What many educational leaders, such as I myself, do, Mr. Kohn and Mr. Glasser, is take the whole—in this case, the classroom—break it down into separate pieces, and look for the piece that needs changing or refining," Principal Macksy explained. "What they usually discern first is the piece called discipline because it sticks out the most. Teachers tend to control their students in the same way that I, as the principal, control teachers.

"For the bureaucracy to function, order must be established, underscored by force, especially in the event of contumacious students or even teachers," Principal Macksy continued. "Few of us think about the schoolhouse as a social organization composed of people who must reason, negotiate, cooperate, compromise, and bargain each day we are together."

"The parts of the school system," interjected the father of scientific management, Frederick Taylor (1911), "such as personnel, machines, methods, and materials are separate and discrete. They are not interactive. When you apply science to the processes of management, we can repair the broken part in the system. In schools, I do indeed suggest you fix the discipline and the children will learn. These other things you speak about are not related to production."

"You just can't say 'fix a part' of the principal, teacher, or the student, Mr. Taylor, and the production line can start up again," Principal Macksy rebuffed. "Principals, teachers, and students are interconnected entities, not discrete ones.

"The transmission of knowledge and skills will be replete with obstacles unless we acknowledge this. We have to stop trying to create science out of what is essentially an art," she cautioned.

"We must understand what we believe about people and their interconnectedness in order to understand the direction in which we are going in achieving school goals. This should be true whether in or out of the classroom. If, as principals, we asked at the teacher interview about the aspirant's philosophy of people instead of the philosophy of education, we might find clues as to whom we want in the schoolhouse guiding our children."

"'The belief persists in this culture that our darker side is more pervasive, more persistent, and somehow more real than our capacity for what psychologists call prosocial behavior,'" said Alfie Kohn (1991). "'We seem to assume that people are naturally and primarily selfish and will act otherwise only if they are coerced into doing so and carefully monitored'" (p. 498).

"If this is so, Mr. Kohn," moaned Principal Macksy, "democracy is doomed and the Goths are the victors!"

"But the point, ladies and gentlemen, is that if we assume that people are selfish human beings only out for themselves, never thinking about the common good," Mr. Kohn explained, "decisions about the classroom constitution will always be based upon control. As a result, the schoolhouse might always be replete with period one teachers."

"In other words," Principal Macksy said, "if a teacher has a basic assumption that all people are naturally born bad or evil and are in need of control, that teacher will govern the classroom with controlling rules. If a teacher thinks that human relationships are based upon intimacy and trust, the students will be invited into the making of those rules.

"What you are suggesting is scary, Mr. Kohn," Principal Macksy reflected. "If I feel I have to control yet don't want to be controlled myself, what does this say about democracy? I will control, but no one will control me. Does that make me a Goth?"

As a result of these assumptions, Dina reflected, like many of the respondents who explored their early schooling, the schoolhouse had become a soulless, autocratic institution, which she at one time in her life simply wanted to escape because she felt controlled. Like respondent Ms. Joan Harvey, it wasn't until college that Dina observed the free flow of ideas and slowly began to participate with those having the ideas. And like Ms. Harvey, Dina wanted an education, but feared school. Was the schoolhouse *the Hatchery* for the production of Goth minions?

"I was yelled at," Ms. Harvey said, "in first grade about pronunciation of the word *island* and never held up my hand again. I can still remember where I was standing, the teacher, the room, and everything about that.

"Later on as I climbed the grade ladder," she recalled, "I was also accused of cheating in English honors, which I did not do and was given an *F* for that quarter. And my math teacher put problems on the board and read a paper while we worked on them in silence in class; I would just call friends at home and have them tell me the answers. No wonder I know nothing about algebra!

"My school time was spent," she concluded, "with friends, playing, as I didn't have to study and my high school years were consumed with being popular, being in cliques, and running the school in our peer group, which was very snobby and exclusive. I studied some but mostly just filled out worksheets; I never wrote a research paper and never researched anything; I wrote a few little five-sentence paragraphs for essays and made *As* in everything because it was so easy. It was a real cultural shock to go immediately to the university and experience actual professors who really excited me with learning. I wanted to know so much more. They didn't try to control me. But how much better my questions would have been if I had been practiced in asking them!"

"And, I, like respondents Ann Mayer and Judy Wright," Principal Macksy jumped in, "became part of the cohort of quiescent students following the rules and doing what I was told. I didn't want to be humiliated. I just wanted to be left alone. I was not one of the students who floated to the top even though I, too, had aspirations."

"I never got the sense, Principal Macksy," Michael Hart interjected, "that any of my teachers had the slightest interest in my opinions about anything pertaining to my classes or school life. I do remember a run-in with a social studies teacher, who falsely accused me of cheating on an assignment and failed me for his class. I failed his class out of indifference inspired by his abhorrent first period teaching.

"He was the worst teacher I ever had," he submitted. "He singled me out for punitive treatment because I had long hair, and in his opinion, a bad attitude. He had no idea who I was and wrapped me up in a tight little bundle of assumptions that removed all chance of my getting anything from his class. Each time I asked a relevant question, he rebuffed me. I still hold him in contempt, especially after having become a teacher myself, and seeing the vile injustice of his practices."

Dina recounted a passage from the 1980 novel *Housekeeping* by Pulitzer Prize–winning Marilynne Robinson. "In the novel," she told the group, "the character Lucille is accused, as Mr. Hart and Ms. Harvey were, of cheating on a test. 'Lucille was astonished to find that the teacher was so easily convinced of her guilt, so immovably persuaded of it, calling her up in front of the class and demanding that she account for the identical papers. Lucille writhed under this violation of her anonymity. At the mere thought of school, her ears turned red. . . . It seemed to us we were cruelly banished from a place where we had no desire to be'" (pp. 78–79).

Why didn't the teacher take the time to understand why Mr. Hart, Ms. Harvey, or the fictive Lucille was thought to be cheating before lashing out with the accusation? Dina asked herself. Yes, she knew students cheated. However, if students do cheat, there is more than one reason. Does any educator take the time to think about what those reasons might be before humiliating a child? Isn't knowing why people do as they do important if you are to educate them?

"I once cheated on a test," Principal Macksy confessed. "Yes, I had studied but I was confident that the person who sat next to me, whom I didn't know, knew more than I did so I stealthily glanced at his paper. I had no idea about his capability but was so diffident about mine that I was willing to cheat. That's what control does to us!

"And the control continued as I became a teacher, only I was the one doing the controlling," Principal Macksy bemoaned, recounting her early experience as a novice teacher. "I tried to break the mold, but it is hard to do when you have been doing something in a certain manner since childhood and have no other experience on which to fall. The Goths were controlling me, but I didn't know that. But at least I tried, as Mr. Trey Pidation did, to stand up for what America stood for."

Her mind then steered her to West Africa where she borrowed Peter Senge's mirror and turned it inward, learning the ways of the Goths but still thinking deeply about the question about democracy that Mrs. Vera Similitude had posed, still thinking about why the part called control is so paramount in the process of teaching and learning and how antithetical that is to democracy and leadership.

FURTHERING THE DIALOGUE

Writer Anton Chekov said, "Man is what he believes" (Morris, 1999, p. 41). Philosopher Tom Morris (1999) suggested that your beliefs are what guide you throughout the day. How would you prepare to ascertain the sum total of your beliefs and values and the beliefs and values of the people with whom you work in order to make a decision about whether you wanted to continue working within a specific schoolhouse? How would you go about establishing the nexus between a philosophy of people and a philosophy of education?

How does what you believe about people influence your everyday dealings with them? Can there be democracy when no one trusts each other? When you applied for an educational position, can you remember if you were asked about your philosophy of people?

Case Study 5

WHO IS THE SCHOOLHOUSE REALLY ABOUT?

Tyro teacher Dina Macksy meets Goth leadership at a faculty meeting.

"It happened deep in the tropical rainforest of Sierra Leone where I had my first teaching assignment at a boy's secondary school in the chiefdom of Jimmi Bagbo," Principal Macksy told the group at the round table. "I was a Peace Corps Volunteer. After undergoing several months of inchoate training *on being a teacher* by the United States government, I moved forward to being a teacher.

"I was proud to be a teacher," she recalled. "I thought I knew enough about what to do in the classroom because I had seen my teachers do it. How hard could teaching be?

"I promised myself, like the teachers I had experienced, that I would not control, intimidate, or humiliate my students. I would find ways for students to engage in the classroom conversation without fear. In my classroom, my students and I would practice democracy through debate, cooperation, negotiation, and consensus.

"As my teachers before me, I was thinking about *students* as something that one places collectively on a grid and not *students* who lived within and among the lines the designated spaces. I did not even have the cognition that I was doing this. You probably noticed that I used the phrase *my classroom*.

"On my first day of school," she continued, "as the sun rose over my house with the plaster frontage and corrugated metal roof, I walked across the lateritic road to the school compound. I knew that on this day I would promulgate the free spirit of inquiry and knowledge to my students even though I feared talking in front of a group of people. College had not abated that fear.

"I recalled what Mr. Abe Struse, my physic's instructor, had taught me: that there was always an element of uncertainty in everything we do. Nevertheless, I debunked that theory, knowing that, in the mechanical world, all things can be known if one finds the right key to unlock its mystery. We could solve all problems if they were broken down into smaller parts, just as scientific manager Frederick Taylor proposed and my teachers before me did.

"It just made sense when I had no insight into the big picture of how organizations worked. If a student was disruptive in the classroom, you solved the problem by demonstrating with the stridency of your voice who had the upper hand. Correct the part that was not working and the system refreshed itself, the quest for knowledge continuing as the students moved into a quiescent state.

"So, here I was, walking to school, thinking about how in 1961, Sierra Leone received its independence after 150 years of British colonial rule. I was at the forefront of working with a people who were learning how to practice democracy without foreign domination infringing upon their daily actions. I liked my principal, Mr. Ladderclimber, and quickly dispelled the marketplace gossip that he was only serving his time as an administrator in a primitive village in the bush—this was how my students described the village—in order to advance himself within the governmental hierarchy."

"'You mean he is more interested in furthering his career than he is in improving education for the students?'" I asked Noel Itall, one of the four other volunteers assigned to Jimmi Bagbo.

"'He wants to impress those who hold high governmental positions, hoping that they will recommend him for a job in Freetown,' he told me with great American certitude. 'No African educator here wants to work in a bush village. They all want to work in the capital where they will be closer to the seat of power.'"

"Noel Itall knew this," Dina told the group at the table, "because he was no longer a first year teacher and felt he knew everything there was to know about the school, its teachers, its students, and its principal."

"So I chose not to believe his specious comment, looking forward to working with my first principal on enhancing my rudimentary and, as yet, inchoate teaching skills. In exchange, I would model how Americans practiced democracy in the classroom and then return to America, knowing how much more productive it was empowering students than controlling them.

"Of course, at the time," Dina continued, a smile surfacing across her face, "I really had no strategy for the practice of democracy in the classroom because I had somehow learned democracy through the process of osmosis."

Principal Macksy then related to the listeners at the round table how she was filled with ebullience when two weeks after school started, Principal Ladderclimber announced that there would be a faculty meeting. She had never attended a meeting of teachers and their principal, but she was filled with images of educators in profound discussion pondering how to further the students' quest for open inquiry and knowledge, something she, herself, had never been exposed to in her first twelve years of schooling.

"Maybe at this faculty meeting I will also learn how to be a better teacher, I wrote Mrs. Newman. Initially, I thought I was very good at my new job. My students always seemed to be attentive as I lectured or put notes on the board. Then they all failed my tests. There was a lot of red ink on their papers.

"Analyzing the situation I concluded that I was doing the job of teaching but they were not always doing their job of learning.

"I tried to look at things from the point of view of the students and their relationship to me and my relationship to them and both relationships to the goal at hand. However, I didn't yet know how to leave the mechanical world of predictability and enter the quantum one of interconnectedness. So, I relied on my mechanical thinking to explain what was happening in my classroom. When all the facts were aggregated, I concluded that the reason my students failed my tests was because they did not study hard enough and were attending too many village dances. I became Mrs. Kalashnikov.

"The meeting was held in the principal's office," she continued, "where the American and African teachers sat on hard, wooden chairs set in a straight line in front of Principal Ladderclimber's long, rectangular work table that also doubled as his desk. He had opened all the shutters of the paneless windows, allowing in the flies that buzzed and zigzagged across the room. I remember the moist air adumbrating another afternoon monsoon.

"I will now read from the journal entries," Dina informed the group, "concerning this first faculty meeting where I would learn how to be a good teacher."

The meeting began, Mrs. Newman, when Principal Ladderclimber mumbled, "Are you all here?" As he voiced these words, he did not even look up from the two piles of paper neatly stacked in front of him. He was carefully scanning each piece of paper, his quick eyes in rapid movement over each; scribbling something in red ink at the top of the page, then lifting the sheet diaphanously with the tips of his fingers and adding it to the second pile before moving on to the next piece of paper.

He was doing pretend work, Mrs. Newman. He was nervous and needed something to occupy his time. Why was he nervous? I asked myself. Wasn't he the principal, the man who greeted me each day with such aplomb, and whose avuncular nature made me feel welcome in my new community?

"No, sah," answered Mr. Swarey, the master of history. "We are not all here." Teachers in Sierra Leone are called masters, I learned, Mrs. Newman, and students are called scholars, a British tradition.

"Who is not present?" Principal Ladderclimber asked, looking up from the pile of papers. "Oh, I see . . . it seems to be the math department. They are always late. You would think that they were not capable of reading the numbers on the clock. Punctuality is important. It is what we teach the boys. We will wait for Abu and Amara."

He hesitated before returning to his pretend work and looked across at the line of masters assembled before him. "But they should be more punctual," he noted, as he peered across at me, his eyes rising above his spectacles.

"Miss Macksy does not permit students who are late into her class," he chuckled. "Maybe we should forbid them from coming to the meeting. But we do operate under a democracy where we are more understanding."

Fifteen minutes and hordes of flies later, the math latecomers, Mr. Abu and Mr. Amara, arrived and seated themselves. "Thank you for attending, gentlemen of the math department," the principal said curtly, slamming his flyswatter down on the table and flicking the squashed remains away with his fingers. "Now I will tell you why I have called you all to my office. It is upon Mr. Dick Siplan's insistence that I make you aware of the following circumstances."

Turning to the Peace Corps master, he said, "I think, Mr. Siplan, you should explain the charges against student George Amadu."

The pedagogues simultaneously turned toward Mr. Siplan. He was a small man with a long, unkempt black beard that fell below his neck. "Yesterday," he began, "I had just started my English class when I saw Chief Prefect George Amadu passing a letter through the window to another student. I walked over to Mr. Amadu and asked him to give me the letter and then to leave the room as he was disturbing my class.

"Mr. Amadu looked at me defiantly. I stood my ground, telling him if he did not give me the letter, he would have to go to Principal Ladderclimber's office. To this Mr. Amadu replied, 'I do not care.'"

Everybody in the room gasped in disbelief. Even the phalanx of flies seemed to momentarily freeze in midair. I thought, Mrs. Newman, the situation extremely grave because students had to be compliant in order for teachers to teach and students to learn. That's why each teacher carried a cane that was used to flog disobedient boys. I too carried it but never used it. Intuitively, I knew that the cane was not a democratic tool.

As the others in the room were recovering from what they had just heard, Mr. Siplan continued with his report. "All right," I said to Amadu, "let's go see Principal Ladderclimber!

"This, sir, is not the first time Mr. Amadu has acted in a disrespectful manner before a master," Mr. Siplan explained, folding his arms across his chest. "My wife has been shown similar insolence by him in her biology class. Also, boys have come to me clandestinely in utter terror of his truculent behavior, reporting that Mr. Amadu has flogged them. I have witnessed him doing this to the freshmen students.

"Mr. Amadu thinks that because he is the chief student prefect at the school he can flog boys anytime he pleases. He also feels that this position entitles him to defy his masters. How can we teach the boys the way of democracy if we are not in control of our students?"

Dina looked up from her reading to explain to the round table members that a prefect was like a student monitor but one with a great amount of power over his peers. She also informed the group at the round table that teachers carried canes in order to instill discipline. As she continued reading, she heard two of the participants who had attended Catholic schools submit that there appeared to be no difference between African teachers and the nuns and fathers at their schools in terms of their ferules.

Dina again read from the journal.

> Principal Ladderclimber, looking up from his pretend work as if he had just heard something he didn't know, asked in a commanding voice, "Why was Amadu's insolence to Mrs. Siplan never reported to me? I am in charge here!"
>
> He turned toward Mr. Siplan's wife. Like robots, the faculty followed in pursuit. "I just . . . just didn't," she stammered, cowering in her chair, her shoulders sagging against the hard back. "I wanted to give him a chance to correct his behavior. He was thirty minutes late to my biology class, sir. I asked Mr. Amadu to leave class since he was so late and was now disturbing others. Mr. Amadu said he wouldn't leave because he belonged in this class even though there was no science laboratory.
>
> "Then he stood in front of the class and made a speech about you, Principal Ladderclimber . . . about you 'not building a laboratory so that the scholars will more fully learn the lessons.' Those were his exact words."
>
> "'This has nothing to do with being late,'" I said to him. "I must admit, sir, I did raise my voice and told Mr. Amadu to leave this room at once. He stood a few moments, glared at me, before leaving."
>
> "It is beyond understanding that you did not report this highly inflammatory situation to Principal Ladderclimber!" said Mr. Abu, one of the tardy math teachers. "Students must be ruled or they will not learn!" His grip around his cane, Mrs. Newman, tightened as he talked.
>
> "But, be that as it may," the principal continued, picking up a fly-swatter and counterattacking the flies assailing his stacks of paper, "I have called you all here so that we may decide together what action should be taken against George Amadu. Mr. Siplan asked that Amadu be punished in some way, but I informed him that the entire staff would have to decide the matter."
>
> His statement both excited and baffled me, Mrs. Newman. First, I thought what a fine lesson this was going to be in democracy in that we were all going to put our heads together and resolve the crisis of a

disobedient student. But then I found myself whispering to Noel Itall, who sat beside me, "I thought it was the principal's job to punish recalcitrant students. Aren't faculty meetings about inquiry and knowledge in order to further the education of our students? I really need help with this. Why aren't we talking about how to make our students pass their tests and listen to us better?

"Sir, does Mr. Amadu have a record of misbehavior?" I diffidently asked the principal, after sharing my thoughts with Mr. Itall. Maybe, I reflected, by breaking the problem of Amadu's negative behavior into parts, they could find the part that was to blame, punish the part, and get on with the school's business of inquiry and knowledge. That's how Sir Isaac would have done it, Mrs. Newman.

Principal Ladderclimber opened a drawer of his desk, producing a long, thin black notebook, engraved in gold letters with the title *Student Discipline Ledger*. Mumbling to himself, he moved his right index finger down the column of names. They were all very neatly spaced, Mrs. Newman. Mr. Bo Rish would have given him a high grade for very neat bookkeeping practices.

"Amadu, Amadu . . . here it is . . . George Amadu, beating another boy: warned. It was for gum chewing that he beat the boy. George Amadu, leaving the compound without an exit pass: warned. He committed that crime twice. They found him in town. I remember telling him if he liked the town so much, he should stay there."

He laughed and the other teachers followed suit. Then I asked, "Was he given any sort of punishment for the other offenses other than warnings? Students have to be punished if they are going to learn. Giving warnings will not produce changed behavior in a recalcitrant student."

"I see it says here he was suspended for some of his crimes for two weeks," Principal Ladderclimber replied blithely, his eyes still fixed on the book. "Yes, that boy has quite a record."

If his record is so bad, why is he still in school? I thought. It was then that I saw images of Mrs. Kalashnikov yelling at me in front of the class for not meeting her expectations regarding the memorization of a poem. She would never have allowed for this and would have rat-a-tatted him right out of the room.

"Why is such a student with a record of misbehavior a student prefect?" I asked. "In a democracy, we do not reward bad behavior."

I hoped that the principal did not think my tone acrimonious or arrogant. I was merely modeling America's spirit of free inquiry that I had learned in college, while attempting to gather all the facts in the case. But I felt myself becoming more audacious and angered because, Mrs. Newman, I wanted to be a better teacher and Principal Ladderclimber was not allowing me to learn how to do this.

"You probably are unaware that Amadu's father, Miss Macksy, is a paramount chief from Salm Malem and holds high office in the government," he informed me, his eyes arresting mine, making me feel uneasy. It was the Kalashnikov stare, Mrs. Newman, the stare that forces you back into General Amygdala's territory.

"He went to Paramount Chief Koker to plead for the boy. Paramount Chief Koker came to me, asking that I allow the boy back to the compound to resume his duties. We must not be drastic with our punishments, Miss Macksy. We must consider all sides and consider the context in which something happens. Isn't this how it is done in America?"

Ignoring the question and shutting my eyes, I said curtly, "Then it is evident, sir, that the only reason Mr. Amadu is in school is that his father is a paramount chief." But I wish, Mrs. Newman, that I had not made that statement. I didn't have all the facts, yet I was quick to rush to a moral judgment without attempting to understand the norms, habits, and beliefs of the culture in which I worked. Examining the facts, before rushing to an opinion, was the way it would be done in America, I surmised.

Principal Ladderclimber, interrupting my thoughts, elaborated upon his remarks. "As I revealed earlier, Paramount Chief Koker visited me and I told him I could do nothing for Amadu. That is, I could do nothing until the boy served the sentence for his crime. After he served two weeks' suspension, I said I would review his case. But Chief Koker did not influence me in any way. Now, let us take a brief break while I put on the fan."

So, we took a break, Mrs. Newman, and I reflected upon my current situation as a teacher and my relationship to the students and the principal. I was the boss in the classroom but because of outside influences, Amadu had power. What was wrong with this relationship? Politics was not part of the educative process.

As I waited for the faculty meeting to start up again, Mrs. Newman, I could not discern why Chief Koker was allowed to interfere in school affairs. As the masters once again took their seats, I erupted. "I vote that we expel Mr. Amadu since it is obvious he is incorrigible. Isn't that why we are here . . . to decide his fate? We can't have students rule the classrooms. They don't know how! That's why they have masters."

"Well, Miss Macksy, let us not allow our passions to overtake our perspicacity," Principal Ladderclimber admonished, in a tone meant to soothe rather than provoke. "We may decide this course later but our primary purpose currently is the pursuit of justice. Is that not what American jurisprudence is all about, Miss Macksy?"

He paused, as if he was gauging the thinking of his teachers, forming judgments in his mind about where they were on *his* page. Maybe, he was just being democratic, Mrs. Newman, and I didn't understand this.

"So now," he voiced phlegmatically, "we will discuss the matter before imposing sentence. Perhaps there was something in the letter that provoked Amadu's anger and made him become offensive to Mr. Siplan without meaning to be offensive. Maybe we should examine the mitigating evidence of this case."

"Even if there are mitigating circumstances," I interjected, now doggedly convinced that this faculty meeting had little to do with education but everything to do with Principal Ladderclimber and his political aspirations, "it cannot explain why he was insolent to Mrs. Siplan."

"But that is another case," Mr. Abu insisted. "We are discussing Mr. Siplan's case. Are we to discuss two cases at the same time? I think we should only discuss one case at a time."

"Both cases have similar results," I snapped, feeling that verbal sparring was not necessary but continuing it anyway.

Mr. Amara entered the discussion, "Does anyone know anything about this letter? To whom was it addressed?"

"Yes, Amara, I quite agree," the principal said, his eyes widening and his face flushing with delight, appreciative of an ally. "We should know what the letter said. Perhaps it had something in it that provoked Amadu's indignation."

"I would like to say that no matter what the content of the letter," Noel Itall advised, "George Amadu was not justified in showing malice toward Mr. or Mrs. Siplan. If we do not severely discipline Mr. Amadu, other abuse will follow by other students. Soon they will all be carrying the canes and not us."

I was proud of my American colleague's statement. The situation had to be handled in an objective manner, employing the scientific method where all observations and results were free of the tempestuous nature of man. It was at that moment that a fleeting thought occurred to me. Maybe the scientific method could not be applied to people working in the schoolhouse.

But as I said, Mrs. Newman, it was a fleeting thought and I had no place in my mind about where to connect this thought. But like all other evanescent thoughts, this one did not become inert. It just stood there in the realm of uncertainty, a realm in which I had scant experience.

"I still am of the opinion that we examine the contents of the letter," Principal Ladderclimber tenaciously announced, standing up, his body leaning into us, the palms of his hands resting firmly on the table. "We must examine all aspects of this case in order to be certain that Amadu receives appropriate representation. Was it not you, Mr. Itall, who said that Mustapha Koroma was not properly represented when it was decided to suspend him for striking Mr. Swarey?"

"Yes, sir, it was me that protested in that case," Mr. Itall answered proudly. "But now I see the error of my ways, wishing now to correct it. I think that Mr. Amadu should have the opportunity to defend himself, but as far as I'm concerned, the letter does not make a difference and should not be entered as evidence."

"I quite disagree," Mr. Abu said. "I do not think we should allow Amadu the right to defend himself because we did not allow Koroma. We must be, above all, fair and consistent. That's why I think we should examine the letter, but not give Amadu the opportunity to defend himself."

The room turned silent until Mr. Siplan asked, "Principal Ladderclimber, why don't we take a vote as to whether Mr. Amadu should be given the chance to defend himself or not? Miss Macksy was not here for the Koroma case and therefore can offer no opinion or vote on the matter. But the others can because they were here." That seemed democratic to me, Mrs. Newman.

"Well, what say you?" the principal asked the masters, scanning the line of chairs and its occupants in front of his table, looking for signs of support. "Should we do that?" All heads but mine nodded their assent.

"Well, then," he summarized, "the case is like this. Mustapha Koroma was not given the chance to plead for himself when committing an act against one of our masters. Some of you objected and said he should have been able to plead for himself. Now some of you think that Amadu should be able to plead for himself. We are going to vote on this matter. All those who think that Mr. Amadu should come here and plead his crime, raise your hands."

Using his right index finger as a pointer, he counted hands. "Well, it looks like the ayes have it so the majority wins," Principal Ladderclimber proclaimed, turning in my direction. "That is very democratic, is it not?"

But not all in the room, Mrs. Newman, were satisfied by the voting outcome. Mr. Abu appeared rankled. "Principal Ladderclimber," he protested, his voice and manner resolute, "the majority, sah, is not always right!"

Mr. Amara nodded his concurrence. "That is right, sah, the majority is not always right."

I was puzzled at this line of thinking. Had Mr. Amara been reading Orwell's book *1984*, where the party would announce that two and two made five and you would have to believe it because that's how those in power programmed the people?

"I have facts to prove my point," Mr. Abu announced, taking heed of the skeptics in the room. "Brigadier David Lansana, our proud head of government, said that there are times when the majority is not right. It was printed in the newspaper."

"Yes, I did see that piece in the *Daily Mail*," the principal exclaimed. "Only I cannot be certain that it is quite what he said. Does anybody else remember reading this statement by the brigadier?" There was no response.

"Then I must make a note to find out precisely what the words of the esteemed brigadier were," he remarked, taking up a pencil and scratching something out on a piece of paper.

When he finished writing, he looked up at his faculty. "Well, I called you here to decide, so we must go by the majority. Let us raise our hands if we want to go by the majority." He counted the number of raised hands. "We all agree except the math department. You are in the minority. You are the negative numbers," he said, proud of his whimsy.

All but the two math masters joined in the laughter. I could hear Mr. Abu murmur under his breath, "The majority is not always right."

"All right, then," Principal Ladderclimber said. "We have voted and the majority has agreed to allow Amadu to plead for himself. Mr. Itall, will you please ask the clerk to escort Amadu into the room."

A few minutes later, George Amadu quickly marched into the principal's office like a soldier on a British parade ground. He briskly advanced around the table, coming to a halt by raising his left leg to almost the height of his waist and then bringing it down in a hard stomp on the ground beside Principal Ladderclimber's chair.

The student, short in stature, gave the appearance of being taller because of his straight, stiff back. The whites of his eyes were icy and ominous. He wore the school uniform: a white shirt and khaki shorts. Unlike other students, his shorts contained a sharp crease down the middle. On his heavily muscled arm was a black band with three white letters that identified him as a prefect. Principal Ladderclimber did not invite him to sit down. Instead, he ordered the boy to remain at attention beside him, facing his accusers.

"Amadu," Principal Ladderclimber snapped in portentous, military fashion, "Mr. Siplan has said that you showed him disrespect yesterday in class by not obeying his orders. What say you to these charges?"

"These are false charges, sah," Amadu superciliously stated, his steely eyes looking up over the heads of the masters at the whirring fan. "Mr. Siplan was absent from the classroom as I received the letter. He should have been in his classroom."

"That is a flagrant lie, Mr. Amadu," Mr. Siplan roared, each of his hands holding tight to his knees as if to restrain further the indignation erupting within him. "I was in the classroom. I asked you to leave because you were disrupting the lesson. I asked you for the letter. You refused to give it to me. You are denying this? Outrageous!"

George Amadu stood his ground. He pinched the bridge of his nose while staring out the open window where a flock of birds hovered over the dense, elephant grass. "Mr. Amadu, I order you to look at me!" Mr. Siplan shouted, exploding again. Amadu didn't move, didn't look once at the reproaching teacher. "You see, Principal Ladderclimber . . . you see how even now he defies me."

Mr. Siplan collapsed into his chair, his face flushing with rage. Dina again heard Mr. Abu muttering under his breath, "The majority is not always right."

It was quiet in the room. Then the student broke the silence, his voice controlled and unwavering as if he were the one in charge of the situation. "The letter was not your property, Mr. Siplan, and that is why you were not permitted by me to have it. It reflects negative opinions about the people of my country . . . the masters, too."

Mr. Swarey, who appeared to be sleeping, jerked open his eyes, the sudden movement taking the flies by surprise and forcing them into momentary exile. "Is that so?" he exclaimed. "Did the letter make reference to me? But I am held in high esteem."

"Yes, sah," Amadu said. "It even said things about Principal Ladderclimber and Paramount Chief Koker as well."

Principal Ladderclimber's forehead furrowed, his eye sockets changing into narrow slits. "About me . . . what did it say about me? This letter, what was it about? Who wrote it? I think it is important that we see it." He turned around, looking up at George Amadu as he spoke.

"It left us, we the masters and scholars at our school with pride, too small," George Amadu opined.

"I think we should have this letter, sah!" Mr. Swarey demanded. There was urgency in his voice. "I must see if the boys object to me in any manner so that I might correct myself and be beloved again."

The principal asked George Amadu if the letter was still in his possession. "It is, sah," he said.

"I really don't see what the letter has to do with Mr. Amadu's flagrant misbehavior in class," I said. "I think by diverting our attention to the letter, we are ignoring the major issue, which is George Amadu's misconduct. And I suddenly feel that we are losing our ability to reason, which is important if we are to conduct ourselves as in a democracy."

"Miss Macksy, what you don't understand is that there may be something in the letter which caused Amadu to be angry and lose his temper," Mr. Abu, exasperated by my comment, explained. "Reason cannot always prepare a path to truth. Sometimes we have to look at alternative paths."

"I do not understand how you can say this, Mr. Abu, when you earlier voted against Mr. Amadu making his case," I countered. But, I knew, no one was listening to me.

"I feel if the letter said something about us we should know what it says," Mr. Swarey reiterated.

"Yes, yes, I quite agree," Principal Ladderclimber said, anxious to have that letter. "The letter mentions me, you say? Get the letter, Amadu."

George Amadu, a wide grin slowly sliding across his face, marched out of the room. Upon returning, he handed a folded, blue aerogram to the principal.

"I see it is addressed to the PCV science teacher," Principal Ladderclimber said. He opened the letter and scanned the contents with his index finger. "I see my name mentioned here," he announced, pointing halfway down the page."

"Principal Ladderclimber, Mrs. Siplan is the PCV science teacher," Noel Itall exclaimed. "Should she not have this letter?"

"Yes, yes, you are quite correct in this, Mr. Itall. However, I cannot just yet do this because my name is mentioned here. . . . It reads, 'Mr. Ladderclimber is a good guy.' Well, the letter cannot be as bad as Amadu has suggested. If you say a person is good, that is a compliment, so you see, Amadu, you have misunderstood this letter's contents."

Attempting a stab at diplomacy, I uttered gingerly, "Of course that statement is true but still the letter is not addressed to you, sir. It is wrong in America to open someone else's mail. Is this not true in Sierra Leone?"

"Yes, yes . . . I know PCV means Peace Corps Volunteer. But it mentions my name. It says right here, 'Principal Ladderclimber is a good guy.'"

Noel Itall implored the principal not to read the letter further. "Sir, that letter is not addressed to you and it is illegal that you read it!"

"No, no, you are not quite correct," Mr. Abu said contemptuously, turning to Mr. Itall. "I think that if what is written in the letter is of a negative quality, we must all read it in order to determine if the wording could have made Amadu lose his temper. As our principal has before stated, we must examine the circumstances that led to this now grave situation."

The room was again silent as Principal Ladderclimber scrutinized the return address on the letter. "I see the letter was written by Mr. Hollis, the former Peace Corps science teacher. Yes, yes, I was fond of him too."

"That's right, sah," Mr. Itall scoffed. "It was written as a personal letter from one PCV to another . . . not to the entire African staff."

"All the boys have read it by now," Mr. Swarey groaned. "I hope it does not list unkind thoughts about me."

I knew it was useless to say anything more, Mrs. Newman. The principal had already decided his next action. For a third time, the room morphed into silence. The masters stared out the glassless windows, watching the birds dive into the elephant grass and soar up into the air with something long, black, and squirming hanging from their beaks. It was probably dinnertime for them.

George Amadu jerked the participants in the room back to his attention. "The letter said negative things about the African staff, sah."

Mr. Siplan, disgusted by the student's prodding, asked the principal if it was any longer necessary to have Mr. Amadu present. Principal Ladderclimber looked around at the other members, but no vote was taken. Without looking up at the student, he told him to leave but stay within the limits of the compound. "I will hold on to this letter," he said.

"But, sah, it does not belong to you!" George Amadu warned.

"Go . . . now!" the principal bellowed, stretching out his arm and pointing his index finger at the door. The student left the room in quick march.

Mr. Siplan then motioned that the meeting be adjourned until the principal had time to read the letter. Again, without taking a vote, Principal Ladderclimber swatted one final fly and declared the meeting over until nine in the evening when we would meet at his house, which like all the masters' quarters, was located on the school compound. Mr. Siplan was vexed. "He has no right to read this letter," he said.

Well, Mrs. Newman, that was that. After all this is Africa, not America. They are only interested in what the letter says about them. We could not go on until Principal Ladderclimber read the letter. . . . Otherwise, we would be sitting in his office with the flies all afternoon and well into the evening when the mosquitoes begin operation Overlord. Who needs it?

Dina stopped reading and addressed the people of the round table. "I remember thinking how disappointed I was with my principal. Principal Ladderclimber, I concluded, was not about education and therefore could teach me nothing.

"Noel Itall was right about him advancing his career. He was weighing his options, knowing that he had to succor both the paramount chief and the foreign teachers on his compound in order to do that. Then, in the private meeting with the paramount chief, he could scapegoat the teachers if the vote went against the student or take credit for it if it didn't. Any way the meeting went, he would win.

"What began as a lesson in democracy slowly dissolved into a lesson in power, patronage, and advantage. I thought I trusted Principal Ladderclimber," Dina reflected, "but found that my trust had been mislaid.

I thought I trusted everyone at the faculty meeting to make rational decisions, but instead learned that two and two could make five. Mr. Abu was right about that, I later discerned. The addition of two numbers could be anything you wanted as long as you inhabited a Goth world.

"My first faculty meeting did not help me to be a better teacher," Dina sighed. "I learned that there could be little education as long as leaders had hidden agendas. George Amadu's teachers had taught him how to manipulate and control situations. The teachers and principal were guiding their students in repeating the cycle of control. Instead of opening the minds of students to knowledge, they were closing them.

"And I followed along. My students had to fear me in order for them to learn. If they feared me, they wouldn't challenge my authority and would learn . . . or at least allow others to learn. I knew that this was myopic thinking but we retreat to what we know when we don't really know. I was the ruler and my students were the ruled. At least I was being honest, I assured myself, and not divisive like Principal Ladderclimber."

"So what happened to George Amadu and the letter?" Mr. Hart asked.

"George Amadu was suspended for two days . . . but kept his job as chief prefect and continued flogging students. Principal Ladderclimber read the letter, as probably did all of the African staff, invited the faculty to his house that evening, providing food and spirits. By the end of the evening, the whole affair was a blur in our minds. But the blur in my mind didn't last for long."

Dialogue 6

HOW DOES CONTROL CREATE TENSIONS BETWEEN THE GOTHS AND DEMOCRATIC ACCOUNTABILITY?

"**S**o that was my first faculty meeting," Principal Macksy said, addressing the participants at the round table. "And as assiduously as I worked at it, I could not file it into any neat category of my mind."

"What you perhaps mean," offered sociologist Willard Waller, "is that you could not take the pieces apart and make them fit neatly together again into a democratic whole that wasn't hostile, distant, and lacking in educational commitment and responsibility."

Dina considered for a moment the sociologist's conjecture. "It did remove me to a bipolar mental state. At one level, during the course of the meeting the principal had asked us to make a decision so I thought the schoolhouse could only be viewed as a place where educators shared in decision making. Out of our interaction would come a decision that would be more meaningful than any decision any of us alone had proposed. We were accountable to each other in making a decision that would impact another human being.

"I was proud that Principal Ladderclimber was practicing democracy and that the rumors about him climbing rungs were false. This is how a democracy should work even though at times I became quite sullen about the lack of *disinterested* thinking at the table where participants seemed more inclined to push forth their own personal agendas. However, even America was still evolving its social experiment in self-government and Sierra Leone was at the very rudiments.

"The people of Sierra Leone wanted democracy," she continued, "but had no tradition of tribes governing together and no sense of accountability to each other like the England of George III or the American colonists. Remember, the American colonists did not rebel because they wanted to be free from England (Johnson, 1997; Wood, 1998). They rebelled because England wasn't playing fair with the rules that the Americans thought they had as Englishmen.

"At another level during the course of the meeting," Principal Macksy explained, "I thought the schoolhouse could only be viewed as an autocracy held together by force, patronage, and the dispelling of rewards. Principal Ladderclimber was going to make it seem as if the faculty was making the decision. In reality, he was going to make the decision that earned him the most leverage with George Amadu's father, who could provide him patronage should the principal need it as he pursued high office in the national government.

"I concluded that if the school was governed by disinterested people who believed only in their personal interests, how far away could the government leaders be from this thought? Of course, I knew that democratic countries were not built overnight. Democratic countries were imbued with strong and capable governments. Their leaders were guided by the rule of law and felt accountable to their citizens, not themselves (Fukuyama, 2011). The government of Sierra Leone was shaky at best when it gained its independence as a free country. As author Mr. David Rosen earlier pointed out, the democracy gradually resulted in a civil revolution underscored by avidity, venality, and child soldiers."

"So you concluded, Principal Macksy," Mr. Waller said, "that the faculty meeting wore the false guise of democracy."

"I did. After my experience at the faculty meeting," Principal Macksy responded, "I realized that there was a link between how people behaved in schools and how people behaved in government, perhaps because one had come from the other. During the two years I was in Sierra Leone, there had been two attempts to overthrow the government. Leaders were not accountable to each other or to the people and were only interested in self-advancement.

"Everything was about control, just as I recalled my own education and some of you recounted yours," she continued. "There were many Mrs. Kalashnikovs who controlled and divided us with fear and favors. I controlled my students just as she did, just as the first period teacher does. I slowly began to realize that we, as educators, play right into the hands of the manipulative Goths and their agents of delusion.

"After the meeting I became so flummoxed with the separation of democracy from education I wondered, did all governments work this way? So, I practiced my free expression rights as stated in the Constitution, a document that I deeply admired, expressing to me the meaning of social individuality and indivisibility in a free nation. I sent my grievances to my mentor, Mrs. Newman. I'll read from a section of my journal during those years."

Mrs. Newman, are democratic values lost in the schoolhouse? What do we do when we one day discover our democratic values are not part of the schoolhouse practice? Do we lose our democracy outside of it? I myself, a pedagogue, find that I am losing my place in my democratic mindset. I, too, threaten contumacious students with the sting of my cane, although I am too cowardly to carry out the threat.

Faculty meetings are a ruse masking the personal advancement of the administration at the expense of those being educated. They numb the pedagogue. I am aghast, Mrs. Newman, when teachers speak not of educational matters but instead choose to focus on the personal ones that in some way reflect individual hubris.

How can students learn when their masters' focus is on playing power games? My first reaction to these problems is confusion. Children who are beaten cannot learn and principals seeking power at the expense of children do not teach. I wonder if educators knew themselves better and could undertake the practice of democracy, if they would be better educators and thinkers.

How can teachers guide their students into the practice of democracy when their guides are like Goths, the Germanic tribe that slowly toppled the Roman Empire because the Romans had forgotten the tenets of the Republic they founded? Rousseau (Rousseau, 1964) said that all things are good until men begin to meddle in them. It was Benjamin Franklin (Isaacson, 2003) who answered, can that be the case because God created, then abandoned us?

But inspired by my democratic beliefs, Mrs. Newman, I race up to my principal's office and share with him my concern. I soon learn that his office is not a haven for democratic ideals. "Kids have to be flogged in order for them to learn," offers Principal Ladderclimber.

"We just can't allow children to run amok in the school, can we, Miss Macksy?" he asks me blithely.

Flogging will not make a student more obedient in class or teach him about democracy, I think to myself. How can a mind that is beaten open itself to creativity and spontaneity?

So what does a teacher, who knows that to preserve democracy one must practice it, do? How do I adapt my ideas of democracy in education with my school's monocratic commitment to ideals both anathema and inimical to it?

Do I pander, Mrs. Newman, to the school's policies of flogging, provide succor for the principal as he furthers his own career in the hope that he will provide advantage for me somewhere else down the line, or take my case elsewhere? To whom am I accountable?

Why doesn't anyone make us aware that education is not really about education and that teachers in the education system are merely pawns of those who hold the power, those people I see as the Goths because they conceive of education as a tool to further their own agendas and ambitions? These Goths wait at the gates, just as the real Goths waited at the gates of Rome and truculently trounced the people.

The modern Goths like Principal Ladderclimber and some teachers are subtler in their approach. They shroud their strategy in the cloth of democracy and unless we are vigilant, they unknowingly use us for their own purposes and not that of the common good. That is what I believe he did at the faculty meeting.

In the mechanical world in which we live, there are always answers. We just have to locate the key that will unlock the door to finding them. I see what schooling in Africa is really about and am even more determined to shower democracy on my students.

Or maybe I am in error about that, Mrs. Newman. Don't all people want the same thing: a feeling of love, safety, and empowerment? Maybe we did have a commonality but just didn't have enough trust in each other to find it. Or maybe we don't know ourselves well enough. Can we know others fully without knowing ourselves? Can we educate another without educating ourselves? Can we locate answers in a mechanical world when we don't have the keys? Maybe the keys we are using are the wrong set.

I believe, at this point of my life, Mrs. Newman, that democracy is about social responsibility and accountability to one another. It is not about individuals meeting their individual needs on the backs of

others. To be a democracy, people must believe in the potentialities
of the individual man, which are linked to the potential of society.

Looking up from her reading and addressing the listeners at the round
table, Principal Macksy said, "And one day, I thought I knew how to
teach students how to activate their voices and perhaps even build trust
among them. As ebullience raced through me, I ran all the way to
Principal Ladderclimber's office, sprinting past the high elephant grass,
the general-use outhouse, and the women selling trays of oranges and
fish squatting at the edge of the school compound.

"By this time I had concluded that my principal knew best about
school operations and he was just exercising his good judgment at the
faculty meeting. After all, like all leaders, he knew things from his high
position that I, as a teacher, was not able to access from mine."

"It seems to me," offered Mr. Reed Linkquich, "that all the deep
reflection you shared with us in your journal resulted in a quiet quies-
cence when something else was really needed. The acceptance of
events was still rooted in your nature."

"Well, it was not as quiescent as you might think, Mr. Linkquich,"
Principal Macksy said. "Of course I say that from retrospect. However,
allow me to continue. Then we will both know if your supposition is
correct.

"Principal Ladderclimber greeted me pleasantly as I entered his
office," she continued. "It was months after the faculty meeting and in
the interim he had been very nice to me. In fact, he ordered a bathtub
all the way from England for my house, which had no plumbing, but it
was the thought that counts. I thought him really a fine man whose
ways I had yet to understand. So, after the preliminary badinage about
this and that, I suddenly mustered the courage to ask him what he
thought about me starting a school newspaper.

"To my complete surprise, Principal Ladderclimber was delighted
that I would take on this extra duty. 'I am pleased that you are thinking
about undertaking this endeavor,' he proclaimed, standing up, smiling,
and coming around his desk. Extending his hand to me, he said, 'The
boys need practice in expressing their opinions. They can do it in this
way. At the same time, they will learn that in a democracy, they have a
right to speak their minds. Not so?'

"I left his office with a sanguine spirit and put together an editorial staff," she told the seminar group. "I was really encouraged when Principal Ladderclimber called the entire staff together announcing his great pleasure at their endeavor. 'It indicates that the school is making rapid strides toward progress,' he said to them. 'I wish you to remember that when you perform your task to the best of your ability as when you are thorough in your work and do it well, you infallibly bring out the best there is in you. Otherwise expressed, you grow more capable and more efficient. You become better and thereby demonstrate your growing superiority and objectivity. And the law is that he who becomes better will attract the better and be given the greater things to do.'"

"Carried forward by my principal's inspiring words," Principal Macksy recounted, "I began the arduous work. Students brought articles daily to the newsroom, consisting of a table and three wooden chairs placed under a tall tree.

"The articles reported on brutish student prefects, flogging, and democracy. This created a tension in me because I, too, carried the threat of the cane around with me."

"But why would you do this if you didn't believe in its use?" Principal Ben Thruitall asked.

"I was advised by my Peace Corps colleagues that if I did not carry the cane in class, the students would think me weak and create discipline problems in the classroom. I knew that holding that cane in my hand meant that I was building power at the expense of building trust. But out of self-preservation, I did as I was advised. I had to balance the tension."

Dina paused for a moment before continuing, inhaling deeply. "As I read the articles submitted by the students, I was beginning to apprehend the brutality of the flogging system. One student, who did not want his name used, submitted this commentary:

The Flogging System

I have noticed a brutal action being practiced at our school. This act is revenging by means of flogging. It is a very cruel act and I think it needs deep consideration. When a student commits wrong, he should not be administered flogging. There are many ways to skin a cat, not only by putting it in a bag.

Mainly brutal students at this school practice flogging. This item recalls to me two events that have recently taken place on the compound. A prefect ordered some boys, whom they call police in the school, to ill-treat a boy at a literary meeting. These police flogged the boy.

In another case, two students stole some provisions from the food store Friday night. One student was caught and mercilessly flogged before being taken to the principal. The principal, after seeing the bad condition of the student, ordered one of his clerks to take him to lockup. Boys on the way attacked them and the thief was again flogged.

A master who wanted to come to the boy's aid was also mercilessly knocked on the head and the clerk was stoned. They nearly killed the boy. Insofar as I am concerned, these boys want to make brutality the rule of life. Let us remember that flogging or fighting was practiced in the olden days and should find no place in our community today.

"I can't help but think as you narrate your story," teacher Michael Hart said, "of what happened in William Golding's (1954), *Lord of the Flies* when the boys were on their own without the guidance of adults and the rule of law went out the window. Reason morphed into fear and fear created injustice as Thomas Hobbes (1996) in his book *Leviathan* predicted it would in a state of nature."

"Well, the teachers and the principal modeled the use of force and the students took it to another level," Principal Macksy responded. "Let me read you another submission where the student advocated the practice.

Our School Is in the Hands of School Police

It is very exciting that this new academic year has brought a new system of discipline in the school. Since the year began, the new masters made an announcement that there must be police prefects. For we Africans, when not forced, will do nothing better and we are mostly afraid of the police for their rough ways of discipline.

After three weeks, some students of the school were appointed police prefects. The main master and his staff ordered that anyone who goes above the rules must be severely dealt with. The rules were that neatness must exist. No playing must be done when students have assembled for eating, devotion, or new calls. Exit passes must be produced any time students go beyond the boundary. Lights must be put off as soon as the bell is gone for assembly, preparation, and school.

During the day, the dormitory must be locked up. And finally, students will not locomote while classes are in session as it is a custom to some boys that when there is not a master in their class, they will go on gallivanting in the corridor.

The first day this announcement was made, the police prefects caught many outlaws and brighter examples were set. We are fighting tooth and nail to undergo these disciplinary measures.

"And so the school had its police prefects whose job was to punish those not obeying the rules," Principal Macksy explained. "But then I saw what happens when power is abused."

She explained to the group that she was walking to her classroom and witnessed George Amadu, the head of the student police force, flogging a new student, who was kneeling before the prefect, his back turned toward him. She immediately ordered him to stop. He did but not before issuing the student one further blow.

"After producing 123 copies of the first school newspaper," she continued, "on the old mimeograph machine sitting on a rotting wooden shelf in an empty room with an engraving on its door which identified it as the library, the paper was ready to be distributed. I was proud of the work the boys had done.

"The paper was filled with articles about the cruelty of flogging but balanced by its need at the school. The schoolboys covered such activities as the visit of a high government official to our campus, a robbery of the food store at the school, and other newsworthy items that the *New York Daily News* would have been proud to print on its pages.

"I knew that the student reporters' work was not up to the coverage of the *New York Times*," Principal Macksy joked, "but one step would lead to another. The cub reporters for now were focused on reporting events in their own backyard, practicing their use of the English language, furthering their own inquiry, and pursuing knowledge for the common good. Jefferson would have been proud of them.

"But accolades were not forthcoming. Instead of encomiums for their sedulous work from Principal Ladderclimber, they received scathing notices proclaiming their work unworthy of dissemination.

"'The paper makes the school look bad, Ms. Macksy,' he decried. 'While I am pleased that you have taken on this endeavor, it is also true that the newspaper should reflect what is good at the school.'"

"What was wrong with the paper," Mr. Hart proposed, "was that there was probably too much truth."

"Principal Ladderclimber specifically objected to the articles about the theft from the food store and the part about the boys flogging the thief until he could no longer walk. He also objected to the flogging articles. 'This makes us look uncivilized,' he exclaimed.

"But it did happen, sir," I told him. "Didn't you say to the students that when you perform your task to the best of your ability, you would infallibly bring all the best there is in you? That's what the students were doing. They used their minds, practiced their language skills, and were open-minded about what they saw happening in the village and school. They didn't put a personal slant on what they reported; they were objective, wrote about what they saw, and checked their facts, putting together a news story. I have been teaching them that they have to leave themselves out of their writing. Did we not do the right thing, sir?

"Of course he concurred," she told the listeners. "After all, he did make the statement I cited. 'Yes, yes, quite so, students have to be objective,' he balked, 'but we want others to see the school in its best light.'

"But sir," I implored, "the boys were reporting on school events . . . like the one written by our editor, Vincent Kawa, about flogging being used as a means for revenging and brutality being the rule of life for some senior prefects. 'Let us remember,' he wrote, 'that flogging was only practiced in the olden days and should find no place in any civilized community nowadays. Only cowards or animals in the bush use force nowadays. Use your brains instead of brutality because flogging creates fear and closes our mind.' This piece shows that the boys are thinking progressive thoughts.

"'No, no. Miss Macksy, we cannot undo years of tradition,' Principal Ladderclimber persisted, unrelenting in his opinion of the newspaper. 'Flogging must continue. It cannot be seen in a negative light.'

"The editorial staff was quite upset when the newspaper was banned from distribution," Principal Macksy said, "but I explained to them that the principal knew better than all of them about what is acceptable and what is not. The truth is that I felt like a failure for not standing up for the right of free speech, but self-preservation once again blocked my way. I did what I was told to do. I wish I had stood up for what I believed, as you did, Mr. Pidation.

"Upon exiting Sierra Leone, I concluded that what I had learned in the African schoolhouse would not happen in its American counterpart. Of course, I did forget that it had already happened to me as well as most of you who talked about your early schooling. And you are right, Mr. Linkquich, I acquiesced. But there were teachers who didn't. Let Principal Ann Gagement take us back to America and tell you about Mrs. Megan Chainges."

FURTHERING THE DIALOGUE

What are the forms of control used in American schools? Are these practices antithetical to creating a democratic schoolhouse? Why would Principal Ladderclimber feel such tension at breaking with tradition and disallowing corporal punishment yet feel that the policy made the school appear uncivilized? How can schools today deal with aggression that spreads beyond the classroom through cyber-bullying while democracy requires free speech?

Think about the parallel this case study makes between the people who teach our children and the people who represent us in government. "There was a link between how people behaved in schools and how people behaved in government, perhaps because one had come from the other." How can one produce the other? To whom are teachers and/or principals accountable?

Case Study 6

DEMOCRACY IN EDUCATION CAN BE PRACTICED BY TEACHERS

Mrs. Megan Chainges practices democracy and moves into the sixth period of teaching.

"**O**n our faculty was a teacher who, as part of her teaching assignment, taught three sections of nutrition to high school students," began Principal Ann Gagement. "When I think about great teachers, Mrs. Megan Chainges is always high on my list. I thought of her as a third period teacher who was honing in on teaching methods that worked to increase her accountability to her students and, as a result, enhance their sense of empowerment.

"She ruled her classroom but did not think of students as empty shells. Mrs. Chainges understood that her classroom control prevented them from reaching their potential. She was cognizant that she favored the students that 'gave her no problems.' In her mind, her classes were divided into the troublemakers and the acquiescing. But she also said that she 'just didn't know how to let go of the control.'

"She was married to an army colonel who operated in a very closed organization and expected absolute obedience from his subordinates. Her attempt to search for democratic characteristics in a bureaucracy contrasted sharply with his leadership style and I often wondered about their process of communication at home."

"I wasn't married to the army," Mrs. Chainges said jokingly as she took a seat at the round table, smiling at her former principal. She was well dressed, wore glasses, and her thinning hair was parted in the middle, braided, and tightly coiled in a bun.

"My husband was and it should not bother you that I pursued this search because the army needed clones; the school did not. But when I think about it, my husband and I were fighting for the same thing, the preservation of American democracy."

"I recall at your evaluation conference," Principal Gagement stated, "talking about how reliant your students were on you. You wanted to develop an action plan where—"

"—my students and I could improve our trust between each other, thus *enabling and empowering* their critical thinking skills," Mrs. Chainges interrupted, completing the principal's sentence.

"I knew I lacked clarity after studying the surprised look upon your face when I stated this. What I meant was that I didn't think that my students knew how to think independently. They were so used to having answers given to them that they didn't even try to conjure up answers to the questions I asked. 'You're the teacher,' they said to me. 'Why ask us questions that you already know the answers to?' I didn't like the students who made statements such as this. I included them on my mental list of troublemakers.

"But they were right. Most of my questions were those that only required rote responses. All around me, my colleagues were pouring answers into their heads and their heads were just rejecting them as demonstrated by their test results. Students, I surmised, were not empowered to think by their teachers.

"I was doing all the work in the classroom while my students insouciantly just sat back in their seats, dozing off with open eyes, texting notes on their cell phones that the school rules prohibited from having on campus, completing homework for another subject, or just doodling on the desk I would clean up after they left. All the time I spent in preparation for my lessons was in vain, I told myself. They just didn't care. I didn't know what more I could do. Maybe I should remain a first period teacher and they should continue to sleep, text, or do homework in class.

"So I went around grunting and groaning about what troglodytes my students were. But having this attitude did not help my students or me. Then I began to realize something that I had said earlier . . . all the time spent preparing for *my* lessons. There was no *our* in the *me*.

"I also recalled something you had said, Principal Gagement, at the annual orientation meeting at the start of the school year. It was something about the relational position that defined the teaching-learning system in the classroom. At first, what you said was nebulous to me because I wasn't really listening. As a result of not feeling connected to what you were saying, I acted as my students did and did something more valuable to occupy my time . . . my lesson plans, I think. But suddenly the tape in my mind rolled back and I played it. I heard you saying that teaching is not about them and us. It's a cooperative, non-competitive effort among all of us in the schoolhouse.

"Then one day I asked one of my classes that had a high failure rate on my exams what it would take to have them all pass these exams at a higher percentage level than they were now attaining. I asked this question after I asked them to plot their grades on a graph. It took two days just to work with them on how to do this. After they got the gist of graphing the grades, someone asked what the class average was for each test. We did this together."

"I had been quiet up until the time she said *we* did this together," Principal Engagement explained to the group. "For me, *we did this together* is a code for teacher speak meaning *I* did all the work. So I asked her to describe how *they* did it together."

"I told the class," Ms. Chainges recalled, "that if they wanted to do this, they would have to show me how. 'Oh you know how,' one student said adamantly. 'Stop playing us.' I rebuffed with yes, I knew how to do it, but for once it would be nice if they did some of the cognitive muscle lifting in class. And you know, to my absolute amazement, for once they began exercising their cognitive muscles.

"One of the students walked up to the front of the classroom, the one who said I was playing them, and said to the students—there were thirty-one in this classroom—to start reading out their scores for the first test. Then he assigned a few students to take out their cell phones—he looked at me when he did this, but I nodded my agreement, hoping that you, Principal Gagement, would not enter the classroom—and add up the numbers 'and then divide by the number of scores.' The students were getting into this and not one student was ashamed to tell his score. Maybe they didn't care if they had a failing score, I told myself. I would have, at their age.

"After they figured out the averages for each of their tests, other students began graphing it on the graph paper I had available in the room. When it was over, the *student teacher* glared at me, grinned in an I-told-you-so manner, and exclaimed, 'So you thought we couldn't do it.'

"I corrected him. No, I thought *we* couldn't do it. He thought about what I meant and then asked if there was something else *we* could do.

"It was the eureka moment for every teacher followed by a rapidly humbling one. I heard a student whisper to another that we may not always do our job of learning, but teachers don't always do their job of teaching. I was hurt, really hurt by the accusation only to be saved by the bell.

"As the student who made the statement left, I approached him, thanking him for his candid remark, explaining that I had overheard him. His face reddened and he apologized, but I told him that I detained him because I wanted him to do me a favor. I wondered if he could give me examples of what he meant by his statement and share it with me in front of the class the next time the class met."

"That was a bold move, Megan," Principal Gagement said to the teacher.

"Well, it wasn't done without a scintilla of reflection," she said. "But I figured if they weren't learning, perhaps I wasn't working as hard as I thought. Or maybe I was working as hard as I thought, but the product was not productive to them. And then two questions popped out at me: Weren't they the product of my work? Wasn't it my job to do for them by doing with them? I didn't know what I meant by this but I was willing to pursue the questions.

"The following day, before the class began, I again asked the student who had made his statement if he would do it in front of the class. I didn't want to put him on the spot as I usually did with students in order to manipulate them into paying attention. I had learned this kind of manipulation from the Effective Teaching workshops we had at school.

"The student had thought about his statement because it was fast in coming. Perhaps he had also invited input from other students. He held up his hand and said that he thought that teachers sometimes don't do their job of teaching and that's why students don't learn. 'Sometimes you talk so much,' he said in a timorous voice, 'that it puts me to sleep.

It is not that what you say is not interesting, but you never allow us to participate in the talk. It's almost like you do all the work.'

"I related to what he said," Mrs. Chainges admitted, "because I was trying to move out of the first period teaching Principal Gagement had spoken to the faculty about at the beginning of the year. Accepting what he said, I asked the students what a teacher whom they could learn from would look like. I didn't know where I was going with this but I couldn't stop at that point. I also asked them if they could *in an inoffensive way* develop a list of criteria for this. I don't want to be hurt too much, I said jocosely and they all laughed. But this was not easy even though I subliminally knew that I didn't need this job. My husband's career kept us financially secure.

"It was also at this point," she continued, "that I had the realization that nutrition was too important for my students not to know about it. They would all probably be parents one day and have their own children and what I had to teach was of absolute value. It also had relevance for the obese youngsters in my class.

"Up to now, my attitude regarding my students had been that it was my job to teach and their job to learn. I felt myself changing. I was wasting my time if I could not enhance my connectedness with them. For this to happen, I needed to know how to increase civility and mutuality in the classroom."

"What did these two words mean to you?" Principal Gagement asked.

"By civility I meant that teachers and students had to have the skills necessary to work together in a calm and efficient manner. By mutuality, I meant interactively working together for the benefit of each other and the group. I told them that we were all accountable to each other and to the class as a whole. If we could learn this, their knowledge and mine would be enhanced. But first, I had to know what their expectations of me were.

"I can't tell you how hard it was to ask them that question about their teacher expectations," she related to the round table group. "I shared none of what I was doing in the teacher's lounge. But I continued, not knowing where this path would lead me, reaching the realization that I was trying to replace competition in the form of my control of the classroom with cooperation in the form of building student and teacher confidence.

"After teaching them the correct way to brainstorm including the need to control oneself if one thought an idea funny or stupid—I am using their terms—the responses came.

"Some of the items listed as having value for students were teachers who would let the students give ideas, listen to the students when they were trying to explain something, not talk too much, not have students work out of a *boring* textbook, try different ways to explain something that was difficult, show respect for students, respect the class, maintain student interest, understand that some students didn't work as fast as others, understand student needs, have patience, and use personal stories to explain things. In all, there were about forty items after we eliminated duplicates.

"When the list was complete, I duplicated it for the class and asked that for each item they rate two things. The first thing was to rate the quality of the skill in reference to me on a scale of 1–4: 1 meaning never, 2 meaning sometimes, 3 meaning most of the time, and 4 meaning always.

"But they were also asked to rate on a similar scale of 1–4 if the quality was important to them: 1 meaning the quality was not important, 2 meaning it was sort of important, 3 meaning it was important, and 4 meaning it was very important. So, for example, the students said that sometimes the teacher let the students give ideas and that was very important to them.

"A committee of students compiled the results and reported them to the class with recommendations of areas where the teacher needed improvement and areas in which they valued what the teacher was doing.

"They asked me to leave the room as they did this. Now I know how students feel when we rate them. It was not pleasant."

"Were you apprehensive?" Principal Macksy asked.

"I was just plain scared. Then they invited me back into the classroom and one student reported the results. They were very kind. I was surprised that they themselves sensed how hard this was for me.

"Some of the areas in which I needed improvement, that is, they wanted to see change, were allowing the students to give their ideas, talking less, working outside the text sometimes, making the subject fun and educational at the same time, and teaching the material using different activities.

"Some of the positive work areas were my ability in listening to them when they were trying to tell me something, the fact that I showed them respect, was cheerful, and encouraged them to do their work.

"I thanked my students and told them that I would act on their recommendations but in return they would have to do something for me. I, too, had a recommendation. There was a silence in the room that rarely occurred. I could hear them thinking, so here comes the catch. The catch, I said, was if I do my part, they would have to attain higher grades on tests. Every two weeks we would again return to our graphs and add the new results. Students who were having problems in increasing their scores would share their problems with me or with some of their peers. They agreed.

"This class became my best class because this exercise did more than conjure up a survey of teacher qualities. It encouraged trust between us. For the first time students came to me about a problem they had with some of the learning and I was able to use their frustrations as feedback for what I was doing.

"You had self-initiated democracy in the classroom," Principal Macksy told her. "You looked into the mirror and realized that your controlling system of teaching was not resulting in a system of learning."

"I did look into the mirror," she said. "I also realized that I had to think of people as rational beings who wanted to do their best. I would not have done this exercise with middle school students. For them, their raging hormones outweigh any rationality they might have.

"Well, you all know the rest of the story," Principal Gagement reported to the round table participants. "As a result of her work, the graphs of test scores in her classroom began to look different. Scores were a little higher, though not all students were passing, Mrs. Chainges told me at the next evaluation conference that she felt that her teaching abilities were improving and she was beginning to move into period four.

"You were one brave teacher!" Principal Gagement concluded, talking directly to the teacher. "You were learning how control creates tensions in the classroom. You became the Goth learning to understand the interconnections between the ruler, the ruled, and accountability, and found that learning occurs when the autocratic ferule is put aside."

Dialogue 7

ARE EDUCATION AND DEMOCRACY MORE ABOUT CLOUDS THAN CLOCKS?

Over the decades, Dina witnessed a plethora of roller-coaster attempts to reform the schools. "In 1973, the United States was ranked high in providing high-quality public education (Lessing, 2012). So what happened?

"There was a time," she explained, "during my early tenure as a principal that I was unencumbered by Superintendent Mac Avelli and deleterious, exterior schoolhouse influences. I felt free as Megan Chainges did to lead the change process in my school when there was a need for it.

"I had the freedom to make decisions which would make a difference in my students' education," she elaborated. "I intuitively knew that for students to learn they had to feel in some way empowered. For me to act, I also had to be empowered. For teachers to act, I had to empower them. And we all had to speak to each other without fear of recrimination.

"If teachers and principals were empowered to act collectively, those high scores on high-stakes tests would be achieved as a by-product of sixth period teaching and leadership," she explained. "We in the schoolhouse have one job. That job is to learn how to apply the concept of democracy to the practice of democracy from the time a child begins his formative school years. We would not need reform from the outside if those on the inside had the social and critical know-how and resources to work collectively.

"If Principal Ladderclimber had not allowed his personal motivations to lead him," she continued, "that young Peace Corps teacher could have taken a first step in learning collective leadership. She was primed for it, but he let her down. If we could look into the mirror and see who we are, we would see others more clearly and understand why as educators we too become the Goths. We can all be Mrs. Megan Chainges collectively. It takes little risk-taking steps. It also means we must become *disinterested* leaders.

"Until educators can work collectively," she reflected, "the Goths, motivated by personal gain, will pronounce that it is the teachers who need reforming, or the principals, or the curriculum, or the instruction, or the school governance, or the school structure. But if we all work together on why we are not producing the results children must have to become successful, informed citizens, there will be no need to tell educators what to do.

"It is always a part that is blamed for the system not working as it should," Principal Macksy concluded. "Nobody bothers to ask the people who work in the processes what the problems are and how they could be turned around. But if they did, I am not certain the educators could answer that question. They don't know how.

"Mrs. Kalashnikov would say it is students who don't study that are the problems. The angry parent in my office would say it's the principals who don't allow teachers to remove the disruptive student from the classroom. The first period teacher would say it's the students who don't do their job of learning. Superintendent Mac Avelli would say it is principals like Connie Sensus who can't control discipline problems at the school. School boards would say it's the teachers who allow students to read vulgar books. Is this the model of democracy that we want for our children? If not, why do we allow this kind of finger-pointing?"

"Everybody, both the politicians and those inside the school system, is into the blame and numbers game," Michael Hart admitted. "We all have that mechanical mindset. We fixate on a part of the problem, focus on that part, and forget that there are many parts of the problem that contribute to the whole."

"That was what I did," admitted Trey Pidation, "when I applauded the angry parent's idea about allowing teachers to eject students from the classroom.

"That's what makes Megan Chainges laudable," he admitted. "She dealt with the whole problem, not just part of it. She walked blindly into a situation, not knowing where it would take her, but cognizant of the fact that what she had been doing was not productive for herself or her students. She believed that she could transform them by empowering herself and her students.

"I used to feel empowered, Principal Macksy, but not anymore," the teacher concluded. "Yet, I still have this passion to lift students up from where they are. I have this passion in working with other teachers to do this. But nobody will give me that chance anymore. The Goths do not share my passion to educate thinking human beings. They only want students to be schooled to become like them. Divergent views rock the boat and are unwelcomed."

"Have we really been hatched in a Hatchery?" Principal Macksy asked those at the table. "Or is it just that we are mindless, having been a product . . . or maybe victim of the public school and its philosophy that schooling can be turned into an absolute science where all events are fixed, immutable, and certain? If kids are doing drugs, the schools should develop a drug curriculum, and if kids continue to do drugs, it's the school's fault because the curriculum was a failure. If students drop out of school, it's the school's fault because the teachers are not motivating them. If students are sexually active, it's the school's fault for not creating an effective program of abstention."

"Before you draw that conclusion, Principal Macksy," former school administrator Larry Cuban (1990) remarked, "you might evaluate why we think within the parameters of this mechanical mindset where cause and effect is the modus operandi. If you can nudge Plato away from his argument with his guest speaker at the academy, perhaps he will help us."

And as soon as Dina turned her head and focused up at the cerulean sky, the Greek philosopher appeared.

"I have found in my dialogues with many men," Plato began, carefully adjusting his toga, "that they become flummoxed and agitated with that which they don't understand. They look for a comfortable truism that provides them peace of mind and security. For example, they may fix in their minds that a certain group of people are bad, and those people are pigeonholed in their cerebral schemata as bad. They don't have to examine why they are bad," he continued, "because they have already fixed in their minds their *badness*. The laudable Mrs. Megan Chainges did allow her mind to pigeonhole her into believing that she was doing her job of teaching but that her students were not doing their job of learning. She began to expand the limitations we sometimes place on our thinking. She decided that the students should begin to do more of the intellectual push-ups.

"My student Aristotle," Plato continued, "is responsible for the curriculum being divided into many subjects. He felt if we broke things down again and again, we would discover the unchangeable essence of things. That is why you have your curriculum divided into separate and discrete subjects. And that is why your students fail to see connections between subjects. And that is why Goths think the way they do and want us to think the same way. You can thank him for that!"

As he peregrinated away, the round table participants could hear Plato mumbling, "Hmmmm . . . maybe my student was a Goth!"

"Plato and Aristotle form the basis of the school curriculum and also lay the foundation for educational theory," summarized Mr. Cuban. "Because man has a difficult time adjusting to what he does not understand, he has struggled to find answers which are fixed and immutable and necessary to his security and peace of mind."

"In other words," Principal Macksy concluded, "men think like mechanics, Goths are mechanics and so are some of us because—"

"This mechanical way of thinking precludes school leaders from coming to grips with the *array of interconnections* in school," educator S. B. Sarason affirmed, completing Dina's sentence. "These interconnections are invisible to a mechanical mindset. However, most educational leaders do not or perhaps cannot search within themselves for a new way of conceptualizing how schools function, so they accept the reforms and depend upon their mechanical thinking to solve problems. Find the defective part and fix it, they think. But education and democracy are not mechanical processes."

"Think of philosopher Karl Popper's distinctions between clocks and clouds," said science writer Jonah Lehrer. "Clocks are neat, orderly systems that can be defined and evaluated using deductive methodologies. You can take apart a clock, measure the pieces, and see how they fit together. Clouds are irregular, dynamic, and idiosyncratic. It's hard to study clouds because they change from second to second. . . . One of the real temptations of modern research is that it tries to pretend that every phenomenon is a clock, which can be evaluated using mechanical tools and regular techniques" (Brooks, 2011, p. 166).

"Reforms fail, Principal Macksy," Mr. Sarason added, "because the public has no understanding of the problem. They think of education as a clock. Find the part that needs fixing and the clock will work again."

"There have been so many efforts to change the school," Principal Macksy rued. "These shot-in-the-dark plans included such ideas as year-round schooling, differentiated staffing, minimum competencies, self-paced instruction, competency-based education, management by objectives, high-stakes testing, block scheduling, school choice, charter schools, compulsory education, child-centered classrooms, life-adjustment education, technology, and basic education, just to name a few (Hunt, 2005).

"All you have to do is look at the cover of *Phi Delta Kappan* to discern what the schoolhouse flavor of the month is," Principal Macksy said, chortling. "It is not that any of these ideas are so bad in themselves; what is bad is that so many of our schools take up the charge in order to change without examining the interrelationship of the new overlay to their schoolhouse. Furthermore, what is the purpose of these changes? Are they to make kids smarter, more ethical, better citizens, high-achieving test takers, more enhanced rote thinkers—what is the purpose?"

"Even with all these reforms, everything still looks the same in the classroom," Mr. Pidation sighed.

"*War is a science,*" the Goths again chanted from their space at the table, "*with rules to be applied, which good soldiers appreciate, recall and recapitulate, before they go to decimate, the other side.*"

"War is a science, but education should not be," suggested educator Richard Gibboney (1991). "My analysis of more than thirty school reform efforts between 1960 and 1990 revealed no real reform. What it did reflect were reforms embedded in a '*technological mindset*' that were neither intellectual nor democratic. In the end, those figures hovering over us right now may win because we, the people, fail to question in whose interests they pursue their goals."

"Yes, the Goths know that they could sell most things to the public," said Reed Linkquich, looking at the section of the table where the spectral figures were still chanting, but now firmly conjoined and suddenly seemingly rising. "The public supports them because we have done a fine job in creating individuals with mechanical, reductionist mindsets. A vote for a Goth is a vote for the nonintellectualization of the American society. We as educators are responsible for this. It is our way of thinking that has produced the Goths."

"Sir Isaac Newton told us," Principal Macksy said, "that the universe was like a great clock. When the clock doesn't work up to expectations, you find the piece that is the problem, fix it, and the clock works well again. But when you fix something in this way, you lose your ability to see a whole picture of the way one part connects to another and how all the parts working together create something greater than each part. That is the tic-toc of the clock. Fixing the part does not always fix the whole because unless the connections are understood, the wrong part may be fixed." As she spoke, she now saw the Goths fixed in space above their section of the table.

"The Goths perceive the public as the four blind men perceived the elephant," Mr. Pidation opined, stealthily watching the rise of the Goths. "The blind men had never known an elephant so they concluded it was different things as they felt it. One felt the trunk and thought it was a snake, another felt the elephant's legs and thought it a tree, the third felt the elephant's tail and thought it a rope, and the fourth felt the side of the elephant and thought it a wall. The elephant himself was befuddled at why four men working together could not put all the pieces together to create a tall, grey mammal (Blind man and an elephant, n.d.).

"Like the four blind men," he continued, "it is parts of things, not the whole thing, that the public is capable of understanding. The Goths know that reducing a big problem to a small one is the way their vanguard of snake oil salesmen can sell their product to the public."

"Myriads of marketplace voters laud the simple solutions to schoolhouse problems," added Principal Macksy. "They are simple to understand and shrouded in monosyllabic, prosaic messages that the public understands. For example, include special education and limited-English-speaking students in regular classes so that the former will be more socialized and the latter will learn English. A good teacher can teach anyone, I hear the Goths and their agents of delusion declare.

"But what the public does not know is that their children require more attention and more resources than ever before because they, the public, have ignored them and have asked the schools to bring them up," Mr. Pidation said, looking directly at the Goths, who now loomed over the table like a prodigious, helium balloon hovering over the crowd at a Thanksgiving Day parade. "While schools are being reformed, the number of students graduating high school is declining" (Swanson, 2010).

"And of course we will blame the teachers for not motivating them," he heard the Goths chant from above. "Further, we will raise the compulsory education age and keep those dropouts in school away from the public."

"Aren't detention centers used for this purpose?" Principal Macksy asked, raising her eyes to the voices and shrouded faces that had, over the course of the seminar, finally attained clarity to her.

"Your quick answers for complex problems create further complexity," she said, rebuffing them. "Everybody follows your bandwagon without thinking about the effects of it on education, society, and democracy."

Thinking reflectively, Dina had experienced the toadies of the Goths. They were well equipped to manipulate modern public opinion whether wearing the guise of the blogging furies or hawkers on the street. They knew how to convince the public that their remedy was the cure-all of cure-alls. They knew how to engage the public in the blame game by taking one piece out of the great schoolhouse puzzle and igniting passions around that piece, using words like *high-stakes testing*, *poor teachers*, or *poor administrators*. It all meant that some one person or group was not doing the job of educating the nation's children.

Knowing that the purpose of schools was to preserve democracy, Dina could not ascertain how all those reforms being sold to the public could do this. But she realized that the Goths were moving closer to establishing their objectives! They were currently hovering over her head.

"One reform does not fit all," she said to the seminar group. "But the Goths have carefully crafted their campaigns of calumny. They select the data that support the argument they choose to make, ignoring any contrary research that undermines their facts."

"It's called cherry-picking," said journalist and college teacher Charles Saife. "'Cherry-picking is the careful selection of data, choosing those that support the argument you wish to make while underplaying or ignoring data that undermine it.'

"'Cherry-picking is lying by exclusion,'" he affirmed, "'to make an argument seem more compelling (Saife, 2010, chapter 1, paragraph 42).' For example, President George Walker Bush said that the nation's students were doing better in reading and math because of a bipartisan bill that Congress passed. This statement is an example of cherry-picking because the report highlighted its merits and ignored its flaws."

"In terms of test scores," added educator, Daniel Koretz (2008), "'even though most of us have encountered this process of buttressing a hypothesized explanation by ruling out plausible alternatives, it does not seem to be how most people think about test scores in education. Instead, they most often note one of two factors consistent with some pattern in the scores and then announce that they can explain them' (p. 123) just as President Bush did."

"And after the public applauds the explanation, the reform movement begins anew because the expected hasn't happened," Principal Macksy told the group. "I know that as an educational leader, it is my job to work with teachers on preparing students to question, hypothesize, and theorize."

"We cannot do this," chimed in Principal Ann Gagement, "if most of our creative energies are spent on demanding that teachers teach to the latest reform. It cannot be accomplished by providing rewards for teachers whose students excelled on high-stakes tests and consequences for those whose students didn't. These divisive methods only serve to divide teachers, lower morale, and disseminate rifts in the school culture, which demands trust if education is to occur at high, extraordinary levels.

"Teachers and principals cannot be viewed as empty shells waiting for the next order," she continued. "That is why I look for teachers who have the pedagogical skills to open student minds, are erudite in their subject matter, know that teaching is a collective endeavor of all individuals in the schoolhouse, care about students, and share a passion for democracy in education."

"These are the necessary ingredients for the teaching and learning process to transform students and save the Republic," said Principal Macksy. "With these ingredients active in the classroom and schoolhouse, the student mind will grow, as will democratic engagement. America will have no fear of following the pattern of the Roman Republic, which forgot what it was about as a free state.

"Daniel Webster taught me," Principal Macksy continued, "the two fundamental requirements for people living in a democracy. One was an unconquerable spirit of free inquiry. The second was a diffusion of knowledge throughout the community. He predicted, 'If they fall, we fall with them; if they stand, it will be because we have upholden them'" (Jacoby, 2010, A25).

Dina knew that the important ingredient in saving the Republic was in his words. Free inquiry and the diffusion of knowledge could only happen if positive human relationships based upon trust existed throughout the nation. Lately, she was not seeing that.

"Instead, what we are seeing are events as in Texas," she scoffed, "where a contentious Texas State Board of Education compressed Jefferson's role in American history because of his deism, approving the rewriting of their own version and vision of history in classroom textbooks (McKinley, 2010). On the national level, American presidents have begun to elevate test taking to higher levels because it is an easy sell. Democracy is being eroded because those who lead are bright but not informed and choose to further their own interests rather than the common one . . . the preservation of American democracy.

"Democracy cannot be maintained through a citizenry that knows how to pass a test but lacks the critical thought and caring to preserve it," the principal surmised.

"Why," she asked, "is the use of democratic practices in the schoolhouse never talked about as the way to reform the schools? Is not the public school, as essayist Robert Hutchinson wrote, 'the foundation of our democracy, the guarantee of our future, the cause of our prosperity and power, the bastion of our security, the bright and shining beacon . . . the source of our enlightenment'?" (Goodlad, 1984, p. 3).

"I believe it is," said Thomas Jefferson. "Universal education is what will preserve American democracy. Without an educated public, citizens are fodder for those opting for a system where power belongs to a few. I feel certain that an educated citizenry will adjust the thinking of those in the state called Texas who would deign to malign my contributions to this great nation because my religious beliefs do not conform to theirs."

Dina hoped that the third president of the United States was not overly optimistic. People could be repressed by the subliminal messages and illusions sent surreptitiously from the airwaves weaving their way into the hinterlands of the subconscious mind. This was a new threat and could only be challenged by thinking people who knew that fixing clocks while ignoring clouds was not an answer. She also was aware that nothing would grow because everything stays small when the Goths are on watch.

FURTHERING THE DIALOGUE

A teacher said this to the author of this book: *Cherry-picking is so blatant because everyone is under pressure to look good; manipulating information and numbers is just a given; makes the whole system seem fake, but then, isn't that reflected every day in our culture? Who knows what the truth is when it is buried under so many layers of bias [and] opinions. . . . So how can schools be expected to lay bare [the] truth when so much depends on the so-called success stories?* Thinking about the school system in terms of clouds, clocks, and Goths both in and out of the schoolhouse, how would you respond to her comment? Can disinterested leaders as teachers and principals govern schools?

Case Study 7

DEMOCRACY IN EDUCATION CAN BE PRACTICED BY TEACHERS AND PRINCIPALS

Principal Ann Gagement practices democracy and moves into the sixth period of schoolhouse leadership.

Students, teachers, and principals working together and practicing democracy in the schools are the keys to preserving the American experiment in democracy, Principal Macksy knew. No matter how many laws the Goths enacted and their minions carried forth, they would all fail in the end if people who worked in the schoolhouse practiced democracy and perceived the importance of reinventing democracy from generation to generation, cognizant that there was no implicit formula for doing this.

Even if her school newspaper failed, Principal Dina Macksy knew her students learned that their voices could be threatening and it was therefore important, as teacher Trey Pidation demonstrated and from which teacher Reed Linkquich learned. And Principal Ann Gagement was optimistic each time she saw her teachers developing into democratic leaders as they moved through the periods during their days and simultaneously watched as her own skills as a democratic leader emerged.

All of these individuals would carry their message forward, extrapolate meaning from it, and pass it on to their students. Perhaps their learning would carry democracy forward, quieting those who would take away their voices. Or perhaps they would become more fodder for the Goths if the voices never learned to speak as one in the same way the voices of the Goths did.

"If education is to happen in the schoolhouse and American democracy is to be preserved," Dina said to the round table group, "it is the individuals working in the schoolhouse that must save the Republic from the Goths."

She recounted the time that all teachers in all core departments were required to give the same final exams. Superintendent Mac Avelli wanted to make certain that they were all teaching and testing to the curriculum guides, for accountability reasons, the superintendent told the department chairs. Principal Macksy even had to request that the department chairs turn in copies of the final exam that each of the teachers administered to their classes. Even with this, she did not know if the teachers were following the district mandate regarding testing. However, she did know some were opting to test students in more appropriate ways that were indicative of student learning and practice.

"So why didn't you call those teachers on the carpet?" inveighed Superintendent Mac Avelli, who returned to the table after receiving a text from Principal Macksy that he might be interested in the current exchange.

"Because these were good teachers who did not want children sleeping in Procrustean beds," she snapped, "and I knew your mandate didn't make sense to them. What they taught was congruent with the curriculum, but the way they taught it was different. This difference required different testing measures. I trusted their judgment.

"There was a prodigious distance," Principal Macksy explained sharply, "between the people who issued orders and those who carried them out, Superintendent Avelli. How effectively the results of the orders are carried out depends on myriads of transmissions between and among the people working in the schoolhouse processes. Consulting your chart on the hierarchical order of power in the schoolhouse will not in any way divulge this to you."

"I was a CEO of a large company," the superintendent bellowed, "and what was good for me was good for everyone. Why are you wasting my time with senseless badinage? I have more important things to do than write up principals who waste time on using the schoolhouse to keep democracy alive. In addition, you spend far too much time in this library instead of scouring the schoolhouse for apostates!" With that, he evanesced out of the room in search of those who refused to be cloned.

"Teachers are sometimes just like him," Principal Macksy cautioned the group. "I once asked a group of teachers how they would run a democratic classroom."

"'Having every kid have a say, Principal Macksy!' they roared in unison. 'Are you crazy!'

"This was most decidedly not the response I expected," the principal sighed dolefully.

"'Are you out of your mind!' exploded the chorus of the Closed-Minded once again. 'The concept is a bit chilling.'

"Let me call some of the teachers to whom I asked this question to the table so that they can speak for themselves." The participants at the round table looked around them as teachers from here and there and everywhere scuttled around the library, followed by the wizened librarian who had just awoken from a nap behind the checkout counter.

"Shall I give them name tags?" the librarian whispered, suddenly appearing beside Dina, huffing and puffing away.

"Yes, but don't take too long. They have to get back to their classrooms or Superintendent Avelli will write them up as well."

After a moment's time, in which the teachers settled in their seats and greeted through nods and smiles the other people at the seminar table, one of the disbelievers in democratic classrooms, government teacher Mr. Entrenched, spoke up.

"People not trained in schoolhouse democracy, Principal Macksy, cannot enact democracy," he proffered in an acrimonious manner. "If the kindergarten teachers had trained their students in this direction, we would not have to be so controlling now. But they, too, know that children cannot rule the classroom."

"Rule the classroom!" Principal Macksy reacted, flummoxed at his concept of democratic education.

"Well, yes, isn't that what you want students to do, rule the classroom?"

Principal Macksy was about to correct his thought by inviting Mrs. Megan Chainges into the conversation, but Mr. Entrenched insisted on speaking further. "I heard a Sierra Leone rebel leader say his people were at war because they wanted democracy. He was the one who would give it to them. How does one just give democracy to a people, or a classroom of students? Do we tell the students they are free to do whatever it is that they want? They have no concept of the practice of democracy, just like the African leader who was going to give it to his people.

"Democracy springs from deep-seated ideas about how to live together in society," he continued, "where the natural instinct is for all people to feel free and empowered to do their own thing as long as it does not infringe upon another person's freedom and empowerment. Students have no understanding of the unwritten social arrangements that bind our country together. They don't know how to sacrifice their wants for the needs that will produce the public good. They would rather bring their previous day's anger into the classroom, disrupting the entire classroom with their wanton actions than be civil.

"Society has not modeled civility or mutuality for them," Mr. Entrenched concluded, "and I fear it is too late to do it now. That was the primary school teacher's job . . . and the parents' . . . and society's. Not mine. If we lose democracy, the blame will be with her . . . or him . . . or them. Running a democratic classroom would be chaos and you, Principal Macksy, would demand that we control our classes or out the door we go!"

"You can't give democracy to people like it was something you serve on a platter," Ms. Further Entrenched chimed in. Dina informed the round table group that she also was an American government teacher.

"Democracy is a template for living in a free society," Ms. Further Entrenched continued. "It slowly evolves into a system when people realize that in order to profit from socially living together, they have to have common values and rules that underwrite the practice . . . rules written by the people . . . practiced and tested by them through debate and discussion in their daily lives for transmission to future generations."

"Sometime in our history, we felt that democracy was valuable, useful, and necessary," added the history teacher Ms. Notta Chainjen. "With common rules created by the people, we protected ourselves from those who felt only they should profit from democracy. Kind of like superintendents and principals," she quipped.

Dina ignored the comment. In a democracy, all people should have their say, she stressed to herself. Superintendent Mac Avelli, not concurring with her thought, would have retreated to his office and put a written reprimand for insubordination in the teacher's box.

"But without the constant practice and vigilance," Mr. Entrenched contemplated aloud, "there can be no democracy. Everybody wants freedom because it is, as Ms. Further Entrenched said, a natural right. But they have to know what the rules for freedom are and that is why we have rules in the schoolhouse and a constitution in the country. If students would listen to me as I taught the Constitution, they would understand what those rules are!"

"Is freedom a natural right for our students, as well?" Principal Macksy asked, insisting on reverting to her earlier point.

"Well, maybe not natural and right for our students," the Chorus of the Closed-Minded agreed. "They wouldn't know what to do with it and if they did would use it for their own purposes."

Mr. Entrenched, in an attempt to provide succor for his principal after noting the plaintive look on her face, said, "Look, Principal Macksy, democracy is not something that cannot be practiced in schools. We can teach students the concepts, arrange for them to vote in their popularity contests for student council office, support them in their fight for new dress codes—even though we know that it will get them nowhere—but the practice has to be demonstrated in social situations like after-school sports or debate clubs, not academic classrooms and certainly not within the confines of a bureaucracy.

"How do you suddenly give students democracy in the classroom?" he asked rhetorically. "I feel the question is as absurd as the revolutionary leader in Sierra Leone declaring that he is leading the revolution so that the people can be free.

"Let's face it," Mr. Entrenched sighed, "students want to be controlled. It's all they know. You ask them to choose. Their response is . . . *do it for me.*"

"But you have to look for opportunities where they will not say *do it for me,*" interjected Mrs. Megan Chainges.

"Or like I did," Principal Ann Gagement said. "I was able to enhance my leadership skills by coupling the practice of democracy with the educative process and enter the sixth period of democratic leadership.

"I wasn't thinking about the art or science of practicing democratic education when I first moved into the principal's office," Principal Ann Gagement relayed to the seminar group. "Nor did I think that I could just pick up a book on educational administration that would outline the steps to take. Nothing in my *want-to-be-a-principal* graduate courses prepared me for this.

"What they did prepare me to be was a leader, not unlike Mrs. Kalashnikov, the autocratic classroom leader who told others what had to be done without thinking that those others were more than empty shells. I intuitively knew that *associative living* meant making compromises, but that intuitive knowledge collided with the autocratic leadership that had been imbued in me in my early years of schooling. I was a Goth even though I didn't want to intimidate, manipulate, or have furtive agendas. I knew intellectually the end result of intimidation was fear.

"My long experience as a principal," she continued, "taught me that democracy in the schoolhouse, as well as in the nation, was a pragmatic art, an organic process that demanded flexibility, adjustment, and thoughtful reflection about the interactive nature of people. I could achieve no educational goal without constantly listening to what people were saying while simultaneously monitoring, adjusting, and thoughtfully reacting to them in a reasonable and sensitive manner. Education was a social process with schooling as its template. The template was secondary to the process and had to be malleable enough to support it.

"I watched as many of my teachers grew in the practice of democracy in their classrooms while I lagged behind in leadership of the school, laying a scientific template over an artful environment. I was stymied by the school's need to move forward. I felt like Mr. Linkquich. He learned from his council position how to utilize democratic skills in his classroom although it did not happen immediately. I had still not been able to apply what I saw working when I observed teachers like him moving ahead in democratic practice.

"I knew on an intuitive level," she admitted, "that change was messy and did not work in a lockstep manner. I knew that individuals working together in the schoolhouse brought underutilized knowledge and experience to the table that could provide order to the mess.

"For example, if the teacher, Ms. Macksy, had not given up on the school newspaper, the process of reporting news might have continued *even* under the auspices of censorship. She could still have guided her students in the development of their journalistic skills and critical thought. She could not predict that something positive would not come of it.

"So one day, during my tenure as principal, I received the welcome telephone call that told me that I had received the principalship of the new school to which I had applied. I had done my research about the school before applying for the job and determined that I wanted to achieve in this schoolhouse what last period teachers achieved in their classrooms."

"What do you mean?" Mr. Dewey asked.

"I wanted to lead an interactive schoolhouse where we could all talk to each other. A large problem at this school, I knew, focused on the morale of the teachers and, as a result, the students, and parents.

"During the second phase of the interview process," she recalled, "I spoke with some of the teachers, those who simpered a feeble attempt at welcoming me while others cowered in the corners, eyeing me skeptically. The ones who did speak to me said nothing about the former principal, but I sensed that they were glad that he had left. My research suggested that he undermined, demeaned, and scapegoated teachers."

"I could well understand why they were skeptical of you," Principal Macksy remarked, still reflecting about how her newspaper students were penalized for her inability to move forward the limitations of her own thinking.

"But I used that skepticism to establish a first goal as their new principal," Principal Ann Gagement reflected. "I had to remove the fear from the schoolhouse. Without it, I could not achieve the high standards I demanded of teachers and students.

"So after talking with the superintendent, Connie Sensus, we agreed that one way I could do this was to have the teachers provide me with feedback on my performance (Walker, 1997). My courage to do this came from Mrs. Megan Chainges.

"If I could deduce what the teachers wanted from me and they could deduce what I wanted from them . . . instead of trying to outguess each other . . . perhaps I could begin a process where we would all work together in meeting student needs," I informed Superintendent Sensus.

"For many years, I had provided teachers with feedback on their performances. Why couldn't they do this for me?

"I had moved from telling teachers what to do, to working with teachers on what to do, to role-playing the doing," she continued. "I had tried many ways to seek teacher input but I knew that every time I invited them to help me with something, some teachers thought I wanted to push more work on them.

"Then, like the third and fourth period teachers, I began throwing out what didn't work and using what did work. When teachers worked on committees with me, I did not always make the final decision. If it was a committee project, it had to have committee results even if I didn't agree with the results.

"But I was always up front with committee members," she said to the round table participants. "I always told them that if our results would impact the district, then I would have to consult with the superintendent. That's one reason why I always kept the superintendent in the feedback loop.

"I didn't realize that it would take many months and several false starts to begin a process which would remove fear in a way which worked for me and the teachers. Then one day at a faculty meeting, I announced that I wanted to remove fear from the schoolhouse.

"I just don't seem to know how to do this," I recall saying to them. "Through the grapevine, I heard that many of you are disgruntled. But nobody has sat down with me to discuss this. I know how anxious most of you become during my evaluations of you. From my point of view, I am not evaluating you. I am evaluating your skills at working with students.

"'That may be,' a defiant teacher in the rear of the room said, 'but it's hard to separate our skills from ourselves. Why don't you let us evaluate you? Then you would know how it feels.'

"It was the eureka moment. 'Why not?' I blurted out. 'Why not evaluate me in a manner where I could learn something about how to build trust among all of us?'"

"I do recall my eureka moment," Mrs. Megan Chainges jumped in. "My lesson plan didn't tell me where I was going with it. Like clouds, things in the classroom changed from second to second. Were you as apprehensive as I was? After all, I had tenure. You didn't."

"I thought if we decided on the rules for removing fear, something good could come of it. We live in a free society underscored by our constitution, so maybe we could build trust with rules with which we all agreed. If I wanted to avoid the demise of democracy, I would have to be part of the process.

"At the meeting, I specifically remember *not* asking for volunteers to serve on a committee to remove fear in our schoolhouse," she told the round table members. "Instead, I said that I would post a signup sheet in my office. I would leave it up for a week. This all happened as teachers were being evaluated."

"Why not ask for volunteers at the meeting?" Mr. Pidation asked.

"Because I wanted teachers to reflect and talk among themselves in the sanctity of the teachers' lounge. I was betting on open-minded people being on the committee. I was also glad nobody asked me about the process of building trust because I didn't have any ideas. I thought that if we knew the goals, the inchoate process would fill itself in.

"After a week, names appeared on the list. It was names of people whom I had evaluated as fitting into some of the seven periods of teaching. We began meeting after school. The first meeting was in my office. Ms. Fifth Period asked me if committee members could report back to the faculty the discussion of the meetings.

"'What do the rest of you think?' I asked them. Mr. Sixth Period said if we all reported individually, reports would be different. 'Why not have each of us rotate as secretary,' he advised, 'recording notes on the laptop as we go along. At the end of each meeting, we could sign off on them. Then perhaps Principal Gagement could duplicate them and put them in teacher boxes.'

"We agreed upon this. 'This is a good way to get input from the entire faculty,' Mr. Second Period commented. 'There are some already asking what trick you have up your sleeve.'

"At this meeting, Mrs. First Period immediately assumed control," Principal Gagement recalled to the round table members. "She insisted that we use her classroom for the meeting so that other teachers could come in and watch the process. However, the other members, after much discussion and acknowledgment that this would be a difficult process for all of us, insisted that this would be acceptable as long as the onlookers did not interfere with the proceedings.

"'After all,' Ms. Third Period reminded us, 'they had their opportunity to be on the committee.'

"Mrs. First Period suggested that leadership of the committee was important. It was funny how they all turned to me. Accepting my silence and not waiting for the others to speak up, she then volunteered to lead the group. When there was no objection, she asked the group what traits they thought their principal should have to remove fear from the schoolhouse. She asked me to record them on the laptop as we brainstormed. I had become the first of the rotating secretaries."

"You must have had some feelings about how Mrs. First Period was vying for control of the group," Mr. Hart said.

"I did, but I had confidence that the group would see it as well. I didn't think that listing traits that the principal should have would help to remove fear, but I bit my lip and allowed the process to work for us . . . albeit I wish I knew where it, I, and we were going."

"That all-mechanical thinking was creeping back in," Principal Macksy joked. "It's hard to get rid of the idea that we should be able to predict outcomes all the time. This was a messy schoolhouse with emotions spread all over the place. It would take an array of interconnected happenings to lessen the fear barometer. That's why you had to be part of the process yet still leading it."

"Listed on the board were traits such as fairness and supportiveness," Principal Gagement continued, reflecting upon what she just heard. "We all agreed that these were primary. Some of the secondary traits were having a vision, a sense of humor, high energy, receptiveness, cooperativeness, child-centeredness, organizational skills, dependability, flexibility, even-temperedness, and warmth. In all, we wound up with a list of over fifty qualities."

"How did you feel as they brainstormed?" Mr. Linkquich asked. "Did you feel they were being objective as I did when I served on the city council?"

"They were not being objective. They were looking at me, recalling their former principal, and judging. I was scared. I felt like a target."

"That's how teachers feel when they are evaluated," Mr. Hart said introspectively.

"I know that to be true, so that's why I was concerned that we lower the fear that the teachers were experiencing. When the brainstorming reached the finish line," Principal Gagement continued, "I knew this list would not make a better leader of me. Jocosely, I asked them to think about whether they wanted God at the helm of the schoolhouse. Mrs. First Period glowered at me. She didn't have a sense of humor. But the others did.

"'That is what the list looks like,' Ms. Third Period concluded. 'Maybe we have to pursue another way to do this.'

"'I have an idea,' Mr. Fourth Period offered. 'Since Principal Gagement talks about democracy all the time, let's see how we can practice what she preaches in this process. Instead of listing traits teachers would like to see in their principal, why not make it more active? What if we ask teachers how the principal treats them in terms of qualities we find important and supportive to reaching schoolhouse goals?'

"Again we brainstormed. What do teachers need from the principal? This time a list of questions was developed: Does the principal treat teachers with respect? Does the principal support teachers? Does the principal treat all teachers fairly? Does the principal seek to solve problems before they begin? Does the principal seek new ideas? Does the principal welcome parents? Does the principal respect those from different subject areas? Is the principal enthusiastic about education? In all, there were thirty-nine questions.

"'Why don't we also ask the faculty if these qualities are important to them?' Ms. Fifth Period suggested.

"'This committee is about the principal, not the teachers,' Mrs. First Period insisted. 'We already have a system of evaluation. The principal could use the information against us.'

"Periods Five thru Seven disagreed. 'But for the sake of argument we won't pursue this,' they concurred.

"The survey was administered and the results were analyzed by the math department," Principal Gagement informed the round table participants. "The math teachers concluded that most teachers thought I was meeting their needs.

"The committee members began to think we were all wasting our time. Then Mr. Sixth Period suggested, 'If we want to know what teachers need from the principal, why not just ask them?'

"As he voiced those words," Principal Gagement told the round table members, "I began to think that as teachers got to know me and acknowledged that I was willing to take risks, the fear barometer might begin a downward slope. I also noticed the slight change in the question that Mr. Sixth Period asked. They were no longer looking for qualities they perceived a principal should have, but specific supports that the principal could give them in order for them to improve their job performance.

"So after deciding who would interview which teacher, the process of asking teachers what they needed from the principal started. Two

months later, the committee members returned with these responses
from teachers (Walker, 1997):

> *I need an instructional leader who can teach me new instructional
> strategies.*
> *I need someone who says positive things about teachers to the com-
> munity.*
> *I need someone who can offer me new ideas about educating at-risk
> students.*
> *I need to know where the principal is coming from.*
> *I need a principal who is trustworthy and who I can share my
> thoughts with.*
> *I need a principal who can help me find the resources with which to
> do my job.*
> *I need a principal who will have donuts on the main office counter
> when I come to school every morning because I really like donuts
> in the morning and they help me to begin the day right.*
> *I need a principal who can get me suitable classroom furniture.*
> *I need a principal who will announce my students' birthdays.*
> *I need a principal who can get me a raise.*
> *I need a principal who shares new ideas with the faculty.*

Ms. Fifth Period suggested we develop a survey using these items.
Eliminating duplications, a survey was constructed. The committee
then asked teachers to rank the need as administered by the principal
and rank the importance of each attribute to them. This time teachers
were directed to put their names on the survey although completing it
was voluntary.

"Mrs. First Period and Mr. Second Period balked. 'This will intimidate teachers,' they argued.

"Periods Four thru Seven intervened, while Ms. Third Period
mulled over the matter. 'The principal will not see these surveys,' they
voiced. 'Only we will. The purpose of including their names is so that
people will take it seriously and not ask that the principal supply them
with donuts.'

"That did not satisfy them," Principal Gagement reported, "but at
least they agreed to disagree.

"After the math department analyzed the findings, the results were
categorized into four components (Walker, 1997). First were items that

the teachers thought were unmet by the principal but were not considered important to them as a group. For example, the teachers perceived that the principal participated in student functions such as class meetings, sports functions, and field trips but it was not important to them that a principal do this.

"Second, they felt that some things were not at all important for a principal to do, such as attending all of their department meetings, announcing student birthdays, socializing with the staff on a weekly basis, working with the students in the classroom, getting teachers a pay increase or nice classroom furniture, and meeting with the teachers on a weekly basis. Others said that although they appreciated the principal's support for teacher pay increases they knew that the district was really in control of this.

"Third," she continued, "the teachers perceived forty-one items as important and met by me. Teachers thought that the open door policy encouraged communication and made me more accessible. Being supportive of them, as in backing them up in discipline matters, was important, especially when parents were present. There were other needs that they encouraged me to continue to meet, such as encouraging teachers to seek new ideas, giving verbal praise and positive reinforcement when apropos, leading the organization in producing a school vision, contributing to positive school spirit, and including the teachers in the planning of school policy.

"After moving through the items, the ones that I was really looking for emerged.

"'Four items surfaced as being of paramount importance to teachers and unmet by you,' Mrs. First Period said, looking down at the paper she was reading. She was not sullen with me this time. But, as she read, I felt my heart pounding. Finally, what I was looking for was there but would it be something I was incapable of doing?

"'First, teachers as a group felt that they were not able to speak to you openly without fear of recrimination,' Mrs. First Period explained. 'Second, teachers didn't like it when they had what they thought was a good idea and you threw it back at them and asked them to pursue it. Because you did this, teachers were reluctant to share their ideas with you. Third, new teachers didn't think you were giving them the training they needed in terms of classroom management and instructional techniques. Finally, the teachers felt that, as a group, they needed support groups so that they could meet together and share common problems.'"

"In your mind, were these fair assessments?" Mrs. Megan Chainges asked.

"They were in their eyes and that was what was relevant to me. The first one was the most difficult to accept. My door was always open and I couldn't figure out why they felt this way. In terms of throwing ideas back to the teacher who suggested it, I did do that but I thought I was being supportive. The last two were more objective and I would have to find the time to do it.

"Then a teacher suggested to the faculty that instead of working on all four areas . . . 'we know your time is limited,' she said, 'we should select the one that was most important to all teachers' (Walker, 1997).

"After considerable dialogue, they eliminated three items and brainstormed how they could meet these needs from within the group.

"This left the item that all the teachers wanted to focus on—that the principal and the teachers be able to speak openly without fear of recrimination. This was as important to me as it was to the teachers. If teachers felt fear in speaking with me, they would not take risks in the classrooms. If the teachers were unwilling to take risks, our school would continue to do the same things over and over again, and change would be difficult."

"There would be no reform," advanced Principal Macksy, "and you would never be able to build a democratic community. 'Leadership is often treated as action by the leader directed toward or against others. More appropriately, we should view leadership as interaction between leaders and followers' (Lipman-Blumen, 2005, p. 17).

"What goes on between you and your faculty," she continued, "is perhaps far more significant for the change process (Covey, 1991) than simply what you as principal do to them. In order for change to occur, there has to be this constant communication between you and the teachers, and they have to feel that you are doing this because it is important to them as well as to you."

"This was the difference for me, Principal Macksy, between mechanical and quantum thinking," Principal Gagement said. "I could simply do to them or we could help each other and refine the interconnections between us. I still had to learn what they meant by their statements so, after the meeting was over, I thanked the committee for their work. 'However, I am not certain how to go about this and I will still need your help,' I told them.

"At the next meeting, I announced to the committee members that I simply could not have teachers fear me.

"'They don't fear you,' Mr. Second Period advanced. 'They are intimidated by your role. You have all the power and they feel they don't have any.'

"'Research indicates that a most common restraining force in accomplishing organizational goals is the existence of fear and distrust in the workplace (Covey, 1991; Deming, 1986),' I stated. 'I have to know how to eradicate fear.'

"'Before developing a plan of action,' Mrs. First Period said, nodding in my direction, 'I suggest we change the word *fear* to *trust*. Fear has a negative connotation.'

"'Yes, it would be easier to write a plan about building trust,' Mr. Sixth Period suggested. I noted that, for the first time, Mrs. First Period had said something positive. Maybe she could change.

"At the next faculty meeting, the Trust Committee led the faculty in a discussion focusing on defining trust," Principal Gagement said to the round table group. "The operational definition agreed upon for trust was 'open communications within the professional work community. Open communications meant that teachers and administration could always "put their beliefs on the table" in professional discussion without fear' (Walker, 1997, p. 101).

"They then brainstormed seven behavioral attributes of trust. In other words, what form did trust take? These attributes were welcoming behavior, confidentiality, friendliness, compassion, honesty, loyalty, and supportiveness. What did we have to do as a team to build toward a trusting relationship? What did welcoming behavior, confidentiality, friendliness, compassion, honesty, loyalty, and supportiveness look like when performed by the teachers and me (Walker, 1997)?

"At yet another faculty meeting," Principal Gagement explained, "we asked teachers for examples of what these behaviors looked like to them. We even role-played. For the rest of the years I was at this school, I practiced trust with them in the workplace. We agreed that if they or I had a question, we would ask it. The teachers and I promised to respect the confidentiality of our conversations.

"The one area in which I really changed was listening to teachers who had personal problems," Principal Gagement said to those at the round table. "It had always been my attitude that personal problems should not enter the schoolhouse gate.

"I found out that I was wrong. A teacher weighed down with personal problems can only have a limited influence in the classroom. Therefore, I listened with more acumen than ever before and it really paid off when we were planning school improvement projects. Teachers were more open and giving of their ideas.

"As a faculty, we continued to talk about trust and the way it could be improved. I shared with them something I had read in a book about toxic leadership. In a survey of seventeen hundred MBA students, it was found that there was a 34 percent drop between 2001 and 2002 in the number of students who said that they were *very likely* to look for other employment if they discovered that their values conflicted with the company's. Instead, they said that they would 'advocate alternative values or approaches,' speak up about 'their objections,' and 'try to get others to join them in addressing their concerns' (Lipman-Blumen, 2005, p. 47).

"That's why I suggested to the faculty that we keep the Trust Committee ongoing. I recommended that perhaps the committee could meet with me every month, after obtaining feedback from the faculty, and let me know how the faculty and the principal . . . all of us . . . were doing at building trust.

"I learned, as Mrs. Chainges did, that entering into a two-way dialogue with teachers was difficult but not impossible. I used to think that since teachers didn't know what my job entailed, there could be no real two-way communication. I was wrong. Without the two-way communication, there was no way to keep democracy alive because the fear barometer precludes positive change."

"So what happened with your ranking after the first year?" Mrs. Chainges asked.

"The teachers perceived trust as still being important and checked that it was met by the principal. Once again, the Goths did not win. We kept democracy alive."

"Freedom requires rules," Principal Macksy told the round table participants, "and democracy requires the practice of those rules. One of those rules is free speech. I think, Principal Gagement, that you not only led the faculty in conquering their fear but you also led the faculty in speaking up for what they believed.

"You showed them what free speech looks like and then it was practiced. So why aren't we doing this with our students? That is, why aren't all teachers endeavoring to teach in the sixth period?"

"Instead of teaching students how to take tests, why aren't we teaching them how to question the tests?" Principal Macksy exclaimed. "For example, freedom of speech allows us to question. Why can't our students be educated in this manner, without tearing down the structure built to school them? Why can't we include students in our classroom conversations?"

"I think we already told you, Principal Macksy," Mr. Entrenched averred, "that democracy means that we have to have the critical skills necessary to see through the distortions of truth that today mark political debates. But I don't think our students want to be informed . . . too much work. They prefer being mindless. . . . Thinking is work. They don't want to be included in the conversations. They just want to know what will be on the test and check their Facebook pages."

People's thinking needs to be reconfigured, Dina told herself . . . including her own. She was trying. That's the only way democracy would be reinvented from generation to generation . . . by teachers like Mrs. Megan Chainges and principals like Ann Gagement trying, in order to avoid its demise, to practice democracy in education.

She, too, like Trey Pidation and Reed Linkquich, had advanced through the periods of leadership development. She could now see the Goths. Knowing who they were and what they wanted made her more aware than ever before that democracy must not become a habit of mind. She knew that democracy needs to be practiced in the schoolhouse because the schoolhouse is the nursery that will nurture a democratic citizenry.

Teachers and principals must guide students in its practice, cognizant of the tensions between those who seek to control, social individuality and indivisibility, and collective democratic accountability. They cannot allow their students to fall into the hands of the Goths and their agents of delusion. It is their job to avoid the demise of democracy. Principal Macksy, addressing all of the participants at the great, round table, thanked them for their contributions to democratic thinking. "But will it be preserved?" she asked, rising from her seat and walking to the door. She turned around and saw only an empty table. Would the Goths still be there when she returned to school?

EPILOGUE

Avoiding the Demise of Democracy!

There was a great, democratic country of the near future called America. Its people believed that the ultimate aim in life was happiness. However, they all agreed that to have happiness, one had to live in a democracy.

One sunny day in May, the shrill, clear tone of a clarion resounded throughout this great nation. The citizens of America, hearing this, telepathically ordered their interactive media devices on and watched as their representatives assembled in the great halls of Congress, where they would once again contemplate a question of great importance.

All watched as the speaker of the nation's Congress mounted a platform set up in the middle of the great congressional hall. In a stentorian voice, the speaker asked the representatives of the people, "How can we, the citizens of our country, preserve our democracy in order to remain eternally happy?"

There was a disquieting moment as the representatives of the people considered the question. In addition, the citizens viewing the assemblage on their media devices also contemplated the question. They thought this an important question because they sensed that America was losing its democratic vision. They didn't know why.

The representatives of the people were equally baffled. "Where is our country going?" they asked themselves, scratching their heads. They were aware that each decade, the divide between the rich and poor became deeper and deeper and the middle classes, so important to a democracy, were slowly fading. They knew that the American economy was in decline. It would soon reach a point where it could no longer compete with the economies of other industrial nations. Large numbers of people were unemployed because they lacked the skills to enter the labor market.

Congressional members didn't know why. They didn't know how to analyze the problem even though their grades in school had been high and they had passed the monthly high-stakes tests that their children now took on a weekly basis.

As representatives of the people began addressing the question regarding the preservation of America's democracy and eternal happiness, those citizens watching on their media devices were impressed with the civil manner in which their representatives spoke, listened, and reflected upon what each person said. The people noted that the years of polarization had faded away. Congress had returned to the art of compromise. The episodic outbursts that had so characterized public debate had long ago evanesced.

"Democracy, education, our economy, and social conditions are intricately linked together," a representative began. "But democracy begins with education. Education and the country's future are linked together. Are we preparing our children for the future?

"If our children do not have the critical skills and knowledge with which to address a changing world," he continued, "the living standard suffers and they cannot be happy. We all have witnessed how unemployed masses of people can topple national governments. We are losing our economic edge in the world because our children are not equipped to deal with an unpredictable future. Can that be why the unemployment rate is so high?"

"I think we also have to ask," another said, "if our democracy has become stagnant, never changing and fixed in time. If this is the case," she said, "then the education of our young is also stagnant, never changing and fixed in time. Has education come to this?"

The students listening to the representative who made this statement knew this already. However, they said nothing to disparage the remark because they respected their elders, having learned from them the practice of civility and mutuality.

"Can it be that teachers and principals are trapped in a public school system designed for an earlier era and do not have the skills and knowledge to prepare them for an unknown future?" asked another representative of the people. "Have all the laws we have passed to make schools better failed?

"As a former principal of a school," he continued, "I always had to ask myself why I was so committed to doing a job that no longer had relevance and lacked purposefulness. Was it because each mandate infused new hope into a failing system? Or was it because I was used to doing what I had always done? Perhaps, if I had been schooled to think critically, I might have questioned the mandates. But I needed a job so I said nothing. I lacked the mettle of some of those maverick principals and teachers who alone are trying to design democratic schools and thereby avoid the demise of democracy."

The congressional leader then spoke. "If we can agree that democracy is pragmatic as well as organic, then education cannot be fixed in time," he advised, addressing the former school principal. "The reforms we passed to fix our failing public school system no longer have any connection to preparing students for the challenges of the new world which they will be entering. The reforms were not sustainable and did not last. As a result, we have created a society that is slowly consigning democracy to oblivion."

He stopped speaking for a moment, caught in reflective thought. Then he exclaimed, "Democracy requires a thinking electorate!"

The students at the schools made a mental note of this statement. Maybe that is why so many young people were unemployed. They didn't know how to think. Perhaps industry needed thinking people. If we could think better, a student thought, industry would employ us instead of outsourcing.

"We have been so polarized in our views for such a long time that we have become oblivious as to the true meaning of democracy," continued the speaker. "Our governmental leadership, our educators, and our local communities have become intellectually impotent, toppling America as the educational leader it was scores ago. We have to fix our schools. To fix them, one has to ask the people why we educate children and why we *want* to educate children. We have to have a common philosophy, a national vision about education. To do this, one must take an unbounded view of a future based upon a constantly changing world of knowledge that cannot be fixed in any time period."

"That is why tethering children to standards, curriculum, and accountability movements that do not provide for the growth of knowledge," the former principal said, "will only serve to further push America further backward socially and economically, allowing further polarization of people into two classes . . . those who have and those who don't."

The speaker reflected again on what had been voiced. "I think we can agree that as a Congress, we have taken a first step out of our present dilemma. The people no longer vote into office ideologues who fight for their individual causes at the expense of supporting the struggles for the common good of all people. The people have taken notice of our example and followed suit. As a result of the years of political contention, they have become aware that our democracy is fragile."

"But this one step is not enough. We must now take bold steps to prepare children for the next era," stated another representative, "even though we don't know what that era or the one after that will look like. Yes, bold steps will be required to avoid the demise of democracy."

There was a disquieting moment as the representatives considered what to do to save democracy and again permeate happiness throughout the nation. Disquietude flowed over the nation.

Then a representative stood up from his seat and broke the silence. "Americans must have a common, conceptual understanding of the interrelationships between education and democracy, schooling, and freedom. Once we as leaders understand this relationship, we will also understand why reforms which focus on such movements as standards, accountability, or high-stakes testing will not develop the critical thought necessary to keep democracy alive."

"There was a report written about the skills that will be necessary for the next century," a representative reminded his colleagues. "Let us look for this report. Can any of our viewers help us with this?"

A student called in. "I am a student in the new Public School of Analysis and Synthesis. Our teachers activate our learning by guiding us in problem solving. They do not control us and they are not controlled. I am doing a project about how old-world school teachers will have to give up control of the classroom and allow our minds guided autonomy, if we, the next generation, are to preserve democracy and find jobs."

"Go and find that report," the congressional leader directed. "We will wait."

The student raced from his classroom to his locker. Under stacks of electronic devices, he found the old iPad 25y that contained the necessary information. Racing back to the classroom, he announced to the speaker that he had at hand the information requested. "I have a report, sir, from The New Commission on the Skills of the American Workforce from the year 2007."

"Activate the machine," ordered the speaker.

The student did as directed. "It is ready, sir."

"Please read it for the congressional representatives and all who are watching this proceeding."

He held up the device to the media screen, activating the speech control. "All the evidence," said a voice on the screen, "points to the fact that workers in the twenty-first century 'will have to be comfortable with ideas and abstractions, good at both analysis and synthesis, creative and innovative, self-disciplined and well organized, able to learn very quickly and work well as a member of a team and have the flexibility to adapt quickly to frequent changes in the labor market as the shifts of the economy become ever faster and more dramatic'" (Darling-Hammond, 2010, p. 1).

"Yes, democracy does require an enlightened and flexible mindset," the speaker reflected aloud. "Students must be taught how to expand the limits of their own thinking."

The student clicked off his device, delighted that he was included in the dialogue of the representatives of the people. They were allowing him to think great thoughts, something that the old schools had scant time for because of preparation for the new, weekly, high-stakes national testing program. He was glad that he had transferred to his new school.

"Why can't our schools prepare children in this way?" asked the speaker.

"Because educators have become clones as a result of the reform movements," said the former principal, "and are producing further clones for the marketplace. But it is not the teachers who are the culprits. It is us. We are also clones and lack a national vision about democracy and education and the interrelationship between this, the econo-

my, and society as a whole. As other industrial countries have demonstrated, clones will not advance American industry on the global scale.

"We have to decide if we want to produce children who sleep in
Procrustean beds," he continued, "or children who know how to think
critically.

"Subjecting students to weekly, national tests has only served to
advance an intellectual malaise over our teachers and principals. Yes,
every once in a while we read that maverick teachers and principals
have spoken up and declared openly that the weekly testing program
does not prepare students for the challenges of the socioeconomic
world to which they are headed. 'There is something wrong when all
emphasis is placed on the test,' they proclaim, 'at the expense of the
critical thought necessary for our young to be successful in *their* future
world.' We have not listened to these mavericks. We are the ones who
have become intellectually impotent!"

"So what do we now do?" the speaker asked somberly. Turning
toward the television monitors, he announced, "We will now accept
comments from the audience. We need your help. Democracy works
best when all the people work together for the common good."

The first citizen made the Congress aware that philosopher and
educator John Dewey asserted that the purpose of formal schooling is
transferring the cultural heritage, values, and aspirations from one generation to another. "He reminded us that for democratic thought to
survive, it has to be renewed each generation and practiced in our
schools. Schools should be microcosms of the world the students will
enter," she concluded.

"If we want to keep democracy alive," another citizen voiced, "we
cannot allow opportunists who believe only in their own individual
causes to lead society. We, the people, accept this because we, the
people, no longer know how to *not* accept this. Our skills of critical
thought are slowly eroding. Yet, most of America's citizens would admit
that the education of its children is important. But can they tell you
why? As the American people struggle for an answer to the question,
the nexus between democracy and education will further elude them.

"Why not look at other countries where prosperous economies and
high-achieving students are the rule, not the exception," the citizen
stated. "Let us ascertain what they are doing to keep democracy alive.
Let us look for change that is sustainable and that does not sacrifice

rigorous learning. Let us do it right this time and establish a consensus about how to fix our schools so that all the people can profit, prosper, and live in happiness."

So, Congress sent their best thinking representatives to other countries. They found that in every nation that they visited, very excellent leaders as teachers and principals were necessary to keep democracy alive. From what they saw and heard, they concluded that the quality of schools could be judged by the professional quality of their teachers.

"These countries also recognized that not everybody could become a teacher," commented one of the returning representatives. "Colleges have to accept this fact and provide high standards of entry into teacher training programs," he reported. "Our teacher training programs have to be revamped so that potential teachers learn how to research, diagnose, and prognosticate classroom problems, communicating evidence-based results with other educators. They must be free of the controls that are now put on them in the schools so that they do not fear taking risks. They must be given the time and resources to work with all children. And they must work alongside communities (Sahlberg, 2011)."

In addition, another stated, "Communities must provide the necessary social and welfare services for schoolchildren to succeed. Social and cultural conditions cannot be used as an excuse about why students don't succeed. Government agencies must provide the schools with the necessary services so that equity for all children is guaranteed."

"We live today in a knowledge economy," another returned representative averred. "This simply means that workers who enter it have to be able to think critically, communicate, and be flexible. Teachers have to be able to teach these skills. Colleges have to be able to teach these skills. Government agencies have to support children as they learn these skills. The community has to organize and support what the schools are doing."

"But this will not happen," the speaker advanced, "as long as we sit and do what we have always done. Maverick principals and teachers must continue to keep democracy alive as we reach consensus on a vision for education. We must begin now."

And so a vision was created. From that vision, universities revamped their teacher training programs, setting high standards for admission into them. As more time passed, teachers and principals gained respect from the public for their professionalism, their autonomy, and their accountability. As the economy improved and young citizens attained jobs in it, the government made available funds for the social and economic services that schools needed to do their job of activating lifelong student learning. Communities worked alongside the schools, proud of the way in which teachers were educating their children. Democracy was kept alive and happiness returned to the people because the very excellent democratic leaders as principals and teachers were found.

REFERENCES

Akpan, U. (2008). *Say you're one of them* (Kindle ed.). New York: Little Brown and Company.

Apple, M., & Beane, J. (Eds.). (1995). *Democratic schools*. Alexandria, VA: ASCD.

Bishop, A. (1801). *An oration on the extent and power of political delusion*. Albany: John Barber.

Blind man and an elephant. (n.d.). Retrieved December 6, 2012, from www.wikipedia.org/wiki/blind_men_and_an_elephant

Brooks, D. (2011). *The social animal: The hidden sources of love, character, and achievement* (Kindle ed.). New York: Random House.

Cicero. (1948). *Selected works of Cicero*. Roslyn, NY: Walter J. Black.

Conant, J. (1959). *The new American high school*. New York: New American Library.

Covey, S. (1991). *Principle-centered leadership*. New York: Simon & Schuster.

Cremin, L. (1980). *American education: The national experience, 1783–1876*. New York: Harper & Row.

Cuban, L. (1990). Reforming again, again, and again. *Educational Research*, 19(1), 10–21.

Darling-Hammond, L. (2010). *The flat world and education: How America's commitment to equity will determine our future*. New York: Teachers College Press.

Deming, W. (1986). *Out of the crisis*. Cambridge, MA: Massachusetts Institute of Technology.

de Tocqueville, A. (1969). *Democracy in America*. New York: Doubleday & Company.

Dewey, J. (1916). *Democracy and education* (Kindle ed.). New York: The Macmillan Company.

Dewey, J. (1938). *Education and experience*. New York: Macmillan.

Dreyfus, H., & Kelly, S. D. (2011). *All things shining*. New York: Free Press.

Elam, S. (1984). Anti-American attitudes of high school seniors in the Orwell year. *Phi Delta Kappan*, 65(5), 327–332.

Etzioni, A. (1983). *An immodest agenda*. New York: McGraw Hill.

Evans, H. (1983). We must begin educational reform every place at once. *Phi Delta Kappan*, 64(3), 173–180.

Fukuyama, F. (2011). *The origins of political order*. New York: Farrar, Straus and Giroux.

Gibboney, R. (1991). The killing fields of reform. *Phi Delta Kappan*, 72(9), 682–688.

Glasser, W. (1990). The quality school. *Phi Delta Kappan*, 71(6), 425–435.

Golding, W. (1954). *Lord of the flies*. New York: The Berkley Publishing Group.

Goodlad, J. (1984). *A place called school*. New York: McGraw Hill.

Hansen, D. (Ed.). (2006). *John Dewey and our educational prospect*. Albany: State University of New York Press.

Hobbes, T. (1996). *Leviathan* (Kindle ed.). New York: Oxford University Press.

Honeywell, R. (1931). *The educational work of Thomas Jefferson*. Cambridge: Harvard University Press.

Hopkins, L. (1941). *Interaction, the democratic process*. Boston: D. C. Heath and Company.

Horowitz, A. (2010). *Inside of a dog: What dogs see, smell, and know*. New York: Scribner.

Hunt, T. (2005). *Education lessons from history*. Retrieved September 9, 2012, from http://www.questia.com/reader/action/zoomin

Huxley, A. (1932). *Brave new world* (Kindle ed.). New York: Rosetta Stone.

Isaacson, W. (2003). *Benjamin Franklin: An American life*. New York: Simon & Schuster.

Jacoby, S. (2010, March 19). One classroom from sea to shining sea. *New York Times*, p. A25.

Johnson, P. (1997). *A history of the American people*. New York: HarperCollins E-books.

Kaplan, R. (1997, December). *Was democracy just a moment?* Retrieved July 2, 2012, from http://www.the atlantic.com/atlantic/issues/97dec/democ.htm.

Kenny, D. (2012). *Born to rise: A story of children and teachers reaching their highest potential* (Kindle ed.). New York: HarperCollins E-books.

Knezevich, S. (1975). *Administration of public education*. New York: Harper & Row.

Kohn, A. (1991). Caring kids: The role of schools. *Phi Delta Kappan*, 72(7), 496–506.

Kohn, A. (1993). Choices for children: Why and how to let students decide. *Phi Delta Kappan*, 74(10), 783–787.

Koretz, D. (2008). *Measuring up: What educational testing really tells us* (Kindle ed.). Cambridge: Harvard University Press.

Kurland, P., & Lerner, R. (Eds.). (1987). *The founders' constitution, volume one*. Indianapolis: Liberty Fund.

Lees, K. (1995). Advancing democratic leadership through critical thought. *Journal of School Leadership*, 5(3), 220–230.

Lessing, D. (2012). *Born to rise: A story of children and teachings reaching their highest potential* (Kindle ed.). New York: HarperCollins E-books.

Lindberg, L. (1954). *The democratic classroom*. New York: Columbia University Press.

Lipman-Blumen, J. (2005). *The allure of toxic leaders* (Kindle ed.). New York: Oxford University Press.

Loomis, L. (Ed.). (1943). *Aristotle: On man in the universe*. Roslyn, NY: Walter J. Black.

McKinley, J. (2010, March 13). *Texas conservatives win curriculum change*. Retrieved July 9, 2012, from www.nytimes.com/2010/03/13/education/13texas.ntml

Miller, J. (2011). *Examined lives: From Socrates to Nietzsche* (Kindle ed.). New York: Farrar, Straus and Giroux e-book.

Morris, T. (1999). *Philosophy for dummies*. Hoboken, NJ: Wiley Publishing.

Mueller, H. (1994). *The land of green plums*. Evanston, NJ: Northwestern University Press.

Nichols, J. (2011). *The "s" word: A short history of an American tradition . . . socialism* (Kindle ed.). New York: Verso.

O'Hair, M., & Reitzug, U. C. (1997). Restructuring schools for democracy: Principals' perspectives. *Journal of School Leadership*, 7, 267–286.

Orwell, G. (1949). *1984* (Kindle ed.). New York: Houghton Mifflin Harcourt.

Patrick, J. (2002). *Teaching America's founding documents*. Bloomington, IN: ERIC Clearinghouse for Social Studies/Social Science Education (ERRIC Document Reproduction Service No. ED470040).

Pollard, H. (2013). My teachers. *Back in the Bronx*, 23(80), 13–14.

Ratner, J. (Ed.). (1939). *Intelligence in the modern world* (Kindle ed.). New York: The Modern Library.

Ravitch, D. (2010). *The death and life of the great American school system* (Kindle ed.). New York: Basic Books.

Robinson, M. (1980). *Housekeeping* (Kindle ed.). New York: Farrar, Straus and Giroux.

Rosen, D. (2005). *Armies of the young: Child soldiers in war and terrorism*. New Brunswick, NJ: Rutgers University Press.

Rousseau, J. (1964). *Emile: Julie and other writings*. New York: Barron's Educational Series.

Sahlberg, P. (2011). *Finnish schools*. New York: Teachers College Press.

Saife, C. (2010). *Proofiness: The dark arts of mathematical deception* (Kindle ed.). New York: Viking.

Sarason, S. (1990). *The predictable failure of school reform*. San Francisco: Jossey-Bass.

Schwartz, S. (1972). *Stlyrics*. Retrieved 2012, August, from http://stlyrics.com/lyrics/pippin/warisascience/htm

Senge, P. (1990). *The fifth discipline: The art and practice of the learning organization*. New York: Random House.

Sharlet, J. (2008). *The family: The secret fundamentalism at the heart of American power* (Kindle ed.). New York: HarperCollins E-books.

Smith, B. (1943). *A tree grows in Brooklyn* (Kindle ed.). New York: HarperCollins.

Steinbeck, J. (1961). *John Steinbeck's Nobel Prize acceptance speech*. Retrieved October 17, 2012, from http://www.subtletea.com/johnsteinbeckspeech.htm

Swanson, C. (2010, June 10). *U.S. graduation rate continues decline*. Retrieved from www.edweek.org/ew/articles/2010/06/10/34swanson.h29.html

Taylor, F. (1911). *The principles of scientific management*. New York: Harper & Brothers.

Taylor, R. (1979, February 12). Ban on books "alarming" new trend. *Los Angeles Times*, p. 1.

Ulich, R. (Ed.). (1947). *Three thousand years if educational wisdom*. Cambridge: Harvard University Press.

Walker, S. (1997, March). Customer feedback from the classroom. *Quality Progress, 30*(3), 99–102.

Walker, S. G., & Chirichello, M. (2011). *Principals as maverick leaders: Rethinking democratic schools*. New York: Rowman & Littlefield.

Waller, W. (1961). *The sociology of teaching*. New York: Russell & Russell.

Wilensky, M. (2007). *The elementary common sense of Thomas Paine* (Kindle ed.). New York: Savas Beatie.

Wood, G. (1991). *The radicalism of the American revolution* (Kindle ed.). New York: Vintage Books.

Wood, G. (1998). *Creation of the American Republic 1776–1787* (Kindle ed.). Chapel Hill: The University of North Carolina Press.

Wood, G. (2002). *The American revolution* (Kindle ed.). New York: Modern Library.

Wood, G. (2006). *Revolutionary characters* (Kindle ed.). New York: Penguin Press.

Wood, G. (2011). *The idea of America: Reflections on the birth of the United States* (Kindle ed.). New York: Penguin Press.

ABOUT THE AUTHOR

Sharron Goldman Walker began her experience with education as a Peace Corps Volunteer in the bush of West Africa and has worked as a public school teacher and high school principal for over three decades. Her public school experience extends from kindergarten to twelfth grade in both rural and urban areas. She earned a doctorate in education from the University of Arizona, Tucson.

In 1986, the United States Department of Education awarded her school the National Secondary Education Award. The school was among 286 exemplary secondary schools in the nation receiving this recognition, celebrated by the president of the United States in a Rose Garden ceremony for principals. The Arts and Humanities Council made a film about the school's improvement efforts called *Pride and Power to Win*. *Instructor* magazine featured her as an outstanding principal and she was a Chase Bank Outstanding Principal for the state of Arizona in 1991.

Her first coauthored book, *Principals as Maverick Leaders: Rethinking Democratic Schools*, focuses on the purpose of schooling in a democratic nation. In addition, Dr. Walker has presented workshops nationally on school improvement through democratic methods and written articles about the topic, especially on how principals can use data and the people working in the system to improve their schools.

Active in schools as well as her community, Dr. Walker has served as a mayor and police commissioner in a small town in California. In 1995, the Board of Examiners for Arizona's Governor's Awards for Quality appointed her as an examiner.

She and her husband, Virgil, a retired teacher and administrator, live in Mesa, Arizona, with their two dogs, Harry and George. Sharron continues to write books about the practice of democracy in public schools . . . in order to save the American Republic! Her website on democracy in education is www.letstalkschool.org.

CPSIA information can be obtained at www.ICGtesting.com
Printed in the USA
BVOW07s2259221113

337102BV00002B/6/P